MILL ON THE DON

MILL ON THE DON

THE STORY OF THE DONSIDE PAPER COMPANY

JOHN FEDO

JAMES & JAMES

Acknowledgements

The author and publishers are grateful to the following people and organisations for access to source material and permission to reproduce illustrations: the Local Studies and Business Sections of Aberdeen Central Library and Woodside Library for provision of archival material and permission to reproduce photographs from the George Washington Wilson Collection and other material; David Scudder, Company Secretary, UK Paper, for access to The Donside Paper Company records and minutes of Directors' meetings; and The Donside Paper Company for permission to reproduce photographs of the mill, equipment and personnel.

Title page illustration: *Donside Paper Mill viewed from downstream.*

ISBN 0 907383 39 4
First Published 1993

New photography by Alex Ramsay

Line drawings of local scenes by John Hume

Designed by Tom Cabot

Typeset by Bournetype Limited, Bournemouth

Originated and printed by BAS Printers Limited, Over Wallop, Hampshire

Bound by Hunter & Foulis Limited, Edinburgh.

Paper manufactured by The Donside Paper Company
Text: Consort Royal Silk 170 g/m^2
Dust jacket: Consort Label 125 g/m^2
Endpapers: Consort Royal Silk Tint 170 g/m^2

Published by James & James (Publishers) Limited,
75 Carleton Road, London N7 0ET

Contents

Foreword

OUR CENTENARY YEAR has given us a wonderful opportunity to look back at our proud history and for the first time put on record the fine achievements of our predecessors.

It is impressive to think that hand made papermaking started on our site nearly 300 years ago – eleven years before the Act of Union between Scotland and England. A particularly interesting feature of the history is the close family connection between the founders of the different paper mills in the area: initiated in the 18th century they culminated in the Tait and Donside companies in the second half of the 19th century.

But this is also a modern success story. The increasing sales of the mills on the River Don today represent 15 per cent of the total UK paper industry and are set for even greater expansion. The Donside Paper Company has played its full part in this outstanding achievement. It is now the UK market leader in its chosen field of Real Art paper and Label paper and currently exports 40 per cent of its output.

Donside has over the years maintained continuity of management and a workforce with a long tradition for hard work and loyalty to their mill. Against this background I am proud and privileged to have served Donside for many years as its Manager and to have worked with so many fine people.

In conclusion, a word of thanks to John Fedo who has spent many months researching and writing this book to make it both accurate and interesting.

IAN LAKIN
Managing Director
The Donside Paper Company Limited

CHAPTER ONE

The Lands of Cotton

PATRICK SANDILANDS WAS the laird of the Cotton estate. He was a family man with eight children, a fiery Elder of the Church of Old Machar in Old Aberdeen – he once locked the minister out of his own church – and later became a Deputy Sheriff of Aberdeen. In 1696, only four years after the massacre of the Macdonalds in Glencoe by the Campbells, he started the manufacture of hand made paper at a site on the estate close to the River Don. This was the first recorded papermaking activity in Aberdeen, an area which has since become of major importance to the British papermaking industry.

A branch of the Sandilands family, whose chief was Baron Sandilands of Calder in Midlothian, settled in the North East and purchased the Cotton estate from the Gordons of Cluny in the early seventeenth century. Patrick was the third generation of the Aberdeenshire branch of the family. On his death the estate passed to his son George who sold it in 1748 to Middleton of Seaton who was kin to the Earls of Seaton. George Sandilands then moved to the Bordeaux region of France and pursued the rather agreeable occupation of wine factor.

The estate was sold on to James Jopp who was a spirit and cloth merchant in Aberdeen. Jopp was a prominent citizen in the city and on no less than five occasions between 1768 and 1786 became Lord Provost. He died in 1791

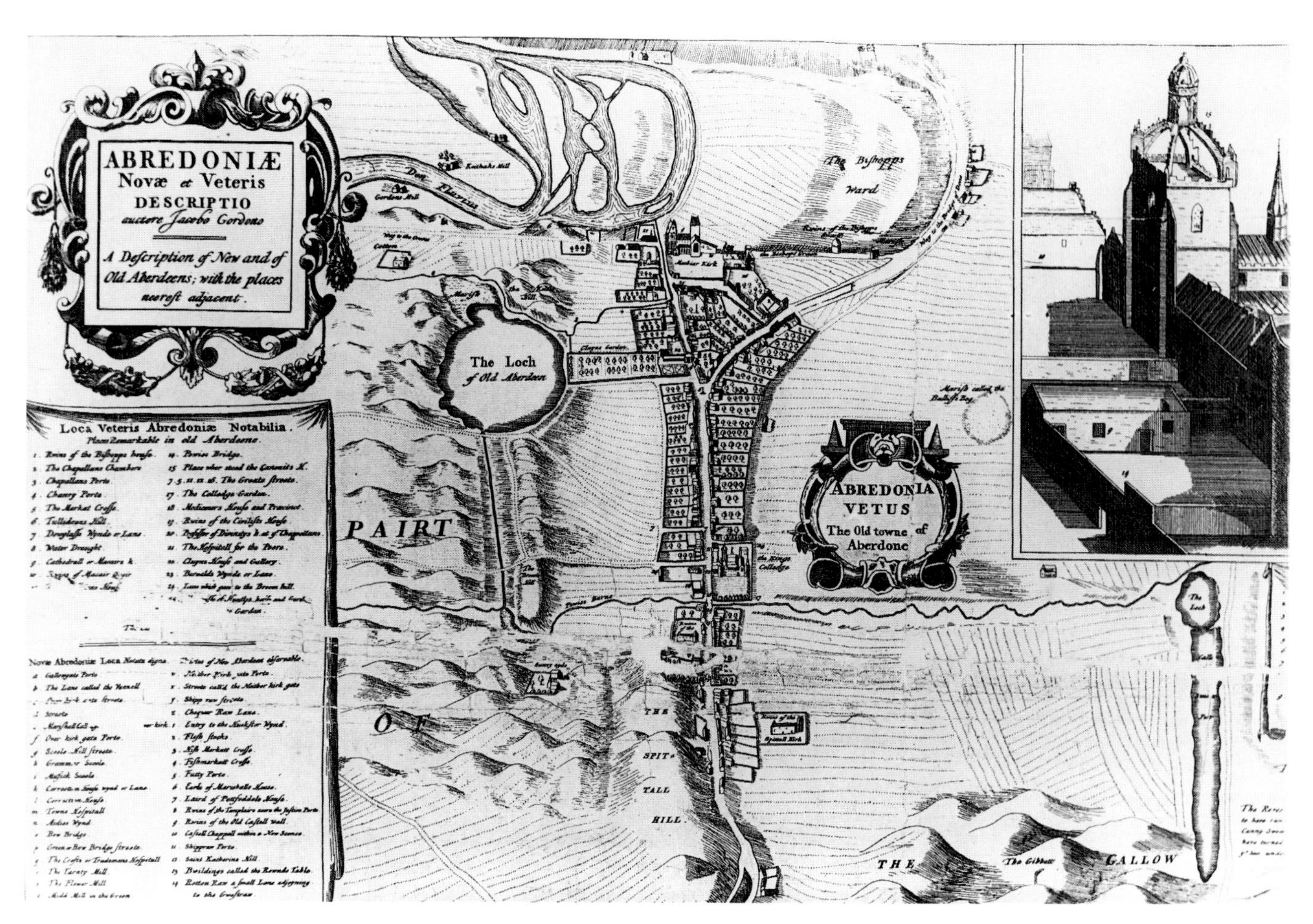

Map of Old Aberdeen, c. 1664. Cotton House and Gordon's Mill are at the top left-hand corner of the map.

and his son, also named James, inherited. He was already in business as a merchant in London and, consequently, disposed of the estate to Forbes of Seaton in 1797. Subsequently it passed by marriage to the Hays of Seaton who owned an estate downstream on the Don. Leases for parts of the land were granted and in certain cases the land was later purchased.

The Cotton estate was situated half a mile west of Old Aberdeen and bounded to the north by the River Don. It extended south to Hilton and west into what was described as 'the most populous and productive area in the district'. In earlier times the surrounding area to the west was called the Lands of Cruives, a name derived from the fishing dykes built across the Don for the purpose of intercepting salmon on their passage upriver. The river became a vital element in the development of industry locally since it provided both an ample supply of water and, by harnessing the water flowing downstream over falls, a cheap source of power for driving machinery.

The original Cruives were constructed just downstream of the present Persley bridge where the Scatterburn, previously known as the Cruives burn, enters the Don. Their sole purpose, clearly described on the maps of the time, was to take salmon and prevent them from passing to the upper reaches of the Don. This was not at all popular with proprietors of land up river from the Cruives who were referred to as the upper heritors. Such was the feeling of outrage that, in 1664, the Earl of Mar, with other noblemen and freeholders upon the Don with about 2,500 horse and foot, convened at Kintore and Hallforest for the purpose of breaking down the Cruives. This army duly marched upon and destroyed the dyke so completely that it was never rebuilt at that part of the river.

The Land of Cruives then became known as Old Cruives and later became the Police Burgh of Woodside in 1868 which was amalgamated into the city of Aberdeen in 1891.

A new construction of Cruives on the Cotton estate at Rapahana one and a half miles downstream from the original dyke was made some time later but certainly before Patrick Sandilands commenced his papermaking venture. In the *Annals of Aberdeen*, published in 1818, a description of the arrangements for the fishings indicates that the dykes across the Don were still unpopular. From the Cruives at Rapahana downstream to Seaton it explains that:

> the fishings on both sides of the river belong to the proprietors of the Cruives. These are formed across the river and the 'hecks' (iron-barred cages) are placed in the gaps as soon as the weather permits after the commencement of the fishing season and taken out when it ends to allow the salmon to make free progress up the river to spawn. The regulation of the Cruives has often occasioned disputes between the proprietors and heritors on the upper parts of the river. Proprietors could regulate the Cruives as they pleased on payment of an annual sum to the upper heritors.

It was alleged that the gaps between the bars in the hecks were reduced so that a two-pound trout could not pass! Despite the compensatory annual payment the upper heritors were never happy with the arrangement.

As industry developed so the need for process water increased and, although river water appeared to be in plentiful supply, agreement for abstraction was often difficult to negotiate. Water intakes to factories and mills generally diverted part of the river flow into a channel or lade. Process water was drawn from the lade and any excess together with waste water was returned to the river downstream. Any difference in water-level flowing in the lade between the points of abstraction and return was used to drive a water wheel and provide motive power for machinery. The raised water-level immediately upstream of the Cruives ensured a larger level difference in the lade which drew water upstream and discharged below the dyke so giving a greater power potential. Negotiations prior to constructing mill lades were often long-winded – in one case the litigation lasted twenty years – and

Brig o' Balgownie, River Don, photographed in the 19th century.

costly. In every case opposition came from the proprietors of the Cruives joined by the upper heritors.

Fishing at the Cruives eventually ceased as the cost of maintenance increased and salmon-netting at the mouth of the Don increased. The gaps where the hecks were placed became widened by erosion and the upstream water-level fell. In recent times the dyke became the haunt of salmon poachers who found the stone crest a ready means of escape from the fishing bailiff! The falling water-level at the mill lade intake led to the design and construction of a new intake independent of the dyke. Finally, in the late 1970s, an army explosives team demolished the Cruives.

Patrick Sandilands established his hand made paper mill on the South bank of the Don at Gordon's Mill opposite the Cruives at Rapahana. A map published in 1661 clearly shows some buildings associated with a Waulk mill – used for fulling or bulking of wool by beating and soaking – were already in existence, having been erected by the previous owners of the Cotton estate – the Gordon family – and he probably adapted these. Sandilands' papermaking venture lasted a mere seven years until 1703, after which Gordon's Mills were used for a variety of enterprises before papermaking was reintroduced in the late nineteenth century.

CHAPTER TWO

Gordon's Mills

WHEN PATRICK SANDILANDS started making paper the mill buildings would have been very basic. Handmade paper required little space and even less machinery. In those days rags provided the necessary fibrous material. These were cleaned, pulped, diluted and stored in a vat. A square wooden frame with a wire-mesh bottom called the 'mould' was dipped into the pulp vat and a quantity of dilute fibre removed in the mould. Excess water drained away leaving a sheet of wet paper on the wire mesh. The sheet was removed or 'couched' by laying a dampened felt cloth on the surface of the paper and applying gentle pressure by rolling a weighted cylinder along the felt. The wet paper then adhered to the felt and was thus removed from the forming wire. Additional water was removed by pressing felt and paper in a flat-plate press. The paper was then removed from the felt and hung to dry in a loft. The skill of the vatman lay in his ability to impart the correct amount of shake to the mould as the sheet was forming to ensure good formation and uniform quality.

When the papermaking venture failed in 1703 Gordon's Mills were converted to cloth manufacture. Production included 'broadcloths, druggets, half-silk serges and damasks and other materials made of wool'. French workmen were engaged for the whitening (bleaching) and scouring of cloth requiring that process. The magistrates of Aberdeen, as trustees of a fund set up for the employment of the poor, entered into a formal contract of co-partnery with Hon. Mr Keith (son of the Earl Marischal) and eight others to start 'the manufacture of woollen goods on a large scale at Gordon's Mills'. To finance this enlarged venture the sum of £600 in capital stock was subscribed.

In 1749 a number of leading citizens of Aberdeen established a company for 'conducting the business on a larger scale'. The manufacture of linen, thread and cloth including bleaching was introduced by the new company Messrs. Leys Still & Co. This company later became Leys Masson & Co. and built premises across the Don at Grandholm where they continued in business until it failed in 1854. In 1859 J. & J. Crombie acquired the Grandholm Mills which continued to manufacture woollen cloth, and gained worldwide fame until in 1990 it fell victim to the recession in the textile industry and was closed.

In the second half of the eighteenth century the site was developed for a number of enterprises which operated concurrently. In 1750 there is a record of an Irishman, Mr Heaney, who had a lease of the bleachfield. In 1762 Gordon's Mill bleachfield was advertising its activities and in the same year a lint mill was worked by a William Innes. From their advertisements it seems that Leys Still were also using part of the site. The diversity of activities recorded suggests an early-day industrial estate!

Towards the end of the century the company Milne & Cruden, which also operated a factory at Spring Garden in Aberdeen, manufactured sewing thread, spun flax and produced silk at Gordon's Mills. It is worth noting that the directors of this company included Mr Alexander Pirie whose principal interest was in the paper mill at Stoneywood three miles upstream on the Don. His eldest son Patrick opted for Milne & Cruden rather than the paper mill and rose to become head of both factories owned by that company which eventually closed down in 1854.

The Pirie family had a further connection with Gordon's Mills when, in 1809, Alexander Gibbon, William and Patrick Pirie were granted a lease for a wool-carding mill. This business, trading as William Pirie & Co, was advertised for sale or lease in January 1842. The notice of sale gives some impression of the growth of the site facilities and equipment over 150 years. There were two water-wheels each producing 80 hp and gas lighting and heating for drying-stoves was installed. Buildings included scouring-houses, dye-houses, carpet-weaving shops, stables, a manager's house, called Don Cottage, and other houses.

By the middle of the nineteenth century trading conditions for the wool and cotton business had deteriorated drastically and Gordon's Mills, with the other mills in the district, were badly affected. The extent of the depression locally can be gauged from an extract of a letter written by Revd Forbes to the *Aberdeen Journal*, the local newspaper. In his letter he cites the fact that, in

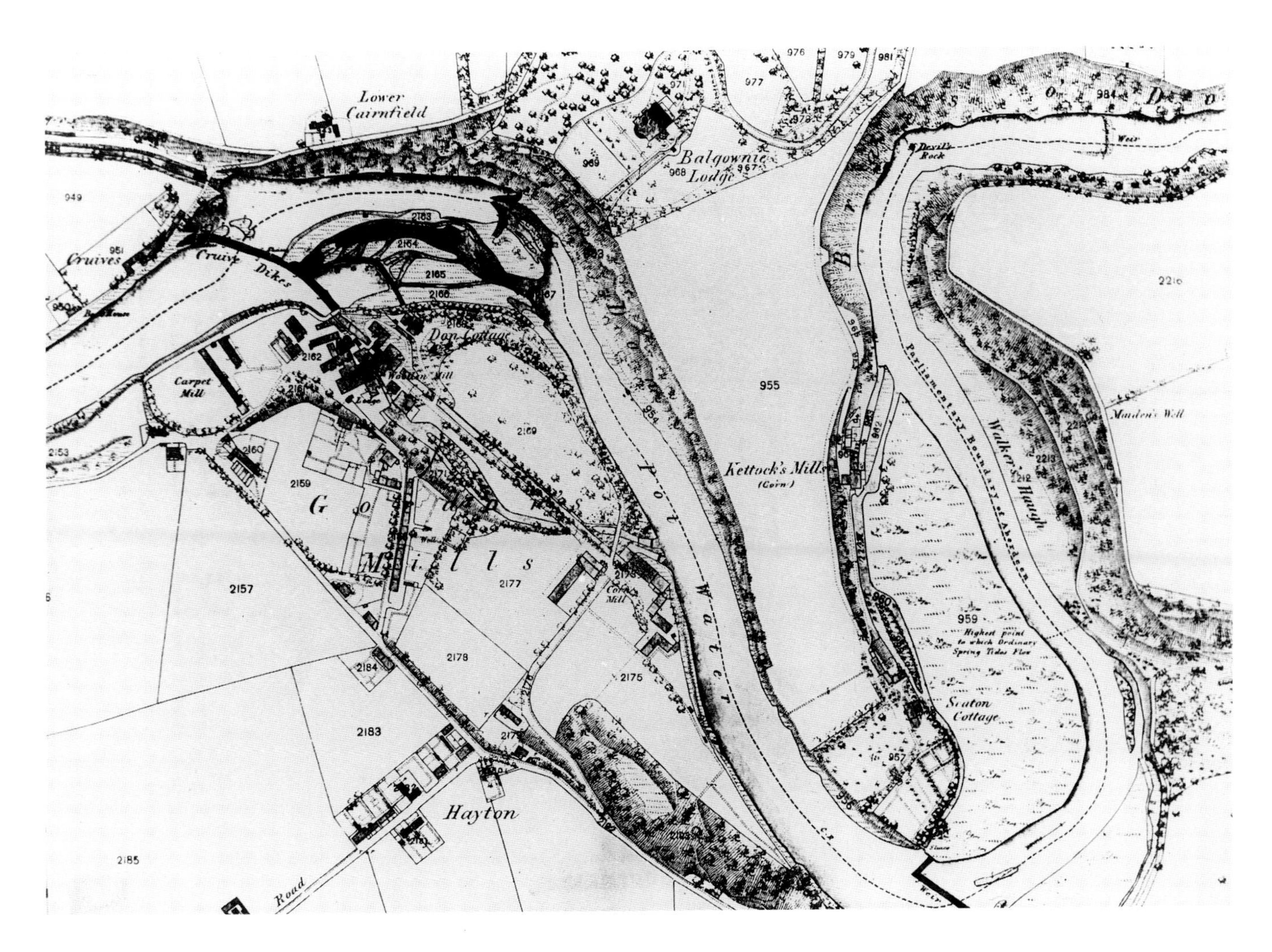

A late 18th century map which shows the development of the site of Donside Mill with the Cruives Dyke and Don Cottage.

1839, all mills were in full operation and giving employment to 2,950 people. In 1848 Grandholm Mill stopped production and 1,334 lost their jobs. It restarted but closed again in 1854 together with Woodside Works with the loss of a further 940 jobs. Added to this was the closure of two mills at Gordon's Mills – the flax and tow works where 260 people went and the wool mill where 420 swelled the unemployment still further. So complete was this disaster that only 50 out of the 2,950 regained employment immediately. However, in 1854 Alexander Pirie acquired Woodside Works for the preparation of rags for papermaking and it employed 400 people. In 1859 James and John Crombie bought Grandholm, providing employment for generations of Woodsiders for the next 120 years.

Alexander Hadden & Co. who had a long history in the manufacture of textiles in the city probably obtained the lease of Gordon's Mills from William Pirie & Co. They set up a wool mill and carpet-weaving factory there in 1875

A view of Donside published by Ackerman in 1849. The Donside Paper Mill now occupies the bank on the right of the picture. St Machar's Cathedral, in Old Aberdeen, is in the background.

Aerial photograph of the Donside Mill taken in the early 1960s. The Cruives and the ruins of Gordon's Mills are shown by the white circle.

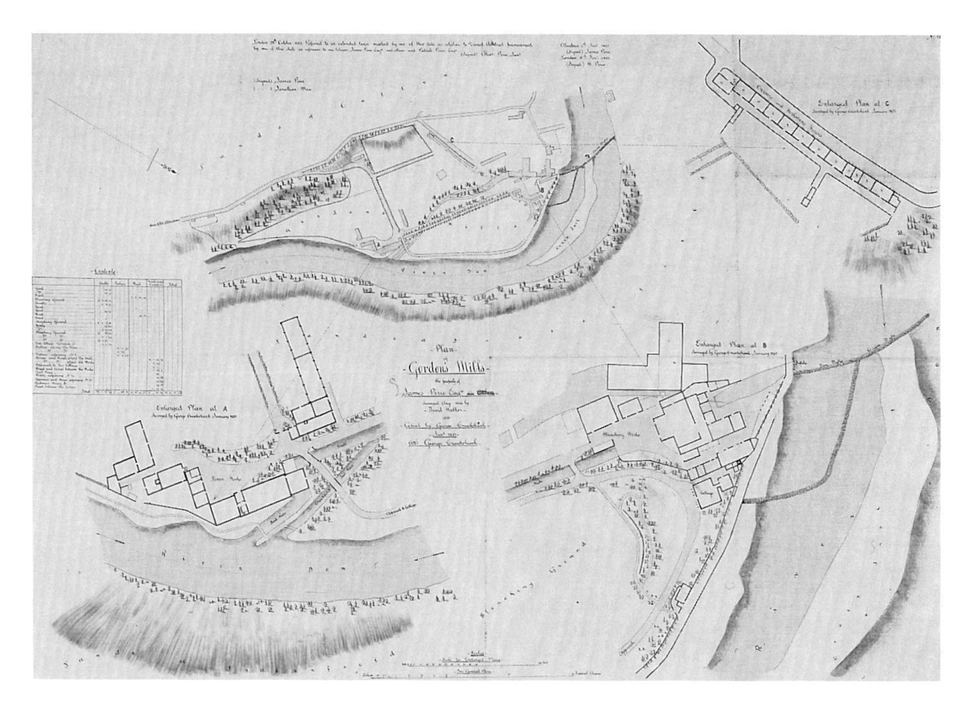

A plan of Gordon's Mills and the Cruives, 1851.

and this continued in business on the site until 1916. Hadden granted a sub-lease to Jonathan Mess and he carried on a business as flour, barley and meal milling and grain merchant until his death in 1866, after which his trustees continued the business up to 1886.

Two years later papermaking restarted on the site, initially using some of the existing buildings. Later, custom-designed stock preparation, machine and finishing houses were constructed. Eventually the old mills near the lade intake were demolished.

CHAPTER THREE

Papermaking on Aberdeen's Rivers

Between Patrick Sandilands' first foray into papermaking in 1696 and the formation of the Donside Paper Company in 1893 dramatic changes in the economy and literacy, both locally and nationally, had taken place. The Act of Union of the Scots and English Parliaments in 1707 was, to put it mildly, unpopular. At that time there was little industry, land management was virtually non-existent and the population was demoralised. An ecclesiastical journal of the time reported that 'the people were poor, ignorant and slothful and ingrained enemies to improvements'. All this was soon to change for the better.

Following the Jacobite risings of 1715 and 1745, when many lairds had been exiled, a gradual return to more settled conditions followed. Pardoned estate owners set about land improvement and started model villages with local industries in order to restore or increase their wealth. The alignment of the Scots and English currencies in 1768 was a strong stimulus in establishing a stronger banking system. Until that time one English pound was worth 12 Scots pounds! By the end of the century there had been a significant improvement in local conditions.

During the nineteenth century came the full range of benefits associated with the Industrial Revolution. Better transport and roads, the steam engine and many other crucial developments came into common use including the continuous papermaking machine, invented by the brothers Fourdrinier and developed by Bryan Donkin. In 1863 the rotary printing press was introduced by an engineer called Applegarth who worked at *The Times* newspaper. This opened up the prospect of large-scale printing operations on an economic basis.

At this time large sections of the populace in Britain were still partly or totally illiterate. The Education Acts of 1870 in England and 1872 in Scotland, with the resulting development of schooling, caused a boom in demand for cheap printing papers. Rags for papermaking were in limited supply. Esparto grass pulp was developed but caused serious pollution problems arising from the boiling and washing processes required. It was because of pollution in the North Esk, a river which runs into the Firth of Forth near Edinburgh, that Alexander Cowan's Valleyfield Mill at Penicuik had to abandon boiling of esparto. They set up a pulp mill at the mouth of the Esk to process their esparto requirements. There the tidal flow dispersed the effluent into the Forth. When improved techniques were developed which reduced the effluent problem Cowans resumed boiling of esparto at Penicuik. Then they began to make paper at the mill near the mouth of the Esk. This mill, named Inveresk, gave its name to the large paper group of which it later became part.

New sources of cheap papermaking fibre were needed. Mechanical woodpulp became available in the 1870s and was the basis for a massive increase of paper for printed material for hundreds of newspapers and periodicals. Development of chemical pulp followed. The yield, per ton of wood, was less than with mechanical pulp but fibre with better strength properties and potential for permanent brightening was produced and used for 'woodfree' paper grades of higher quality.

Paper mills were set up all over the country, many of them small and destined to close or amalgamate. As well as a supply of pulp the other main requirements were a source of cheap power, water in plentiful supply and a reliable and preferably skilled labour force. Consequently papermaking in Britain was concentrated on river systems close to centres of population.

Aberdeen with its two rivers – the Dee and the Don – was a natural choice for entrepreneurs. It had an added advantage as a seaport with excellent harbour facilities. Its proximity to Scandinavian sources of woodpulp became important as did the potential for developing an export trade. The population of the city grew from 27,000 in 1801 to 125,000 in 1891.

After the brief spell of papermaking between 1696 and 1703 at Gordon's Mills on the Don the next mill to be established in the area was at Peterculter on the river Dee some 9 miles from Aberdeen. This was the Culter Mills

Aberdeen Harbour, late 19th century. Foreign woodpulps were among the numerous commodities landed as international trade flourished.

Paper Co., which was established in 1750 by an Englishman, Bartholomew Smith. He started up on the first day of January 1751 (thus proving conclusively that he was English!).

Paper was still produced by hand at this time and the range of products advertised included brown papers, paste board and pressing card for dysters. Mr Smith also gave notice that he would be in Aberdeen on specified days to purchase rags suitable for papermaking. The mill was sold in 1820 for £4,000 to Alex Irvine. It was sold twice more in the years to 1854 at which time the selling rights for the mill's output were taken over by Alex Pirie & Co of Stoneywood in 1856.

In 1865 it was floated as a joint-stock company. Alex Pirie gave up their interest in 1882 and a Mr Geddes, who had been a treasurer at Piries, managed to finance and acquire the mill. Later it amalgamated with the Guardbridge Paper Co. of Fife to form Culter Guardbridge Group. More recently it made coated and fine papers until, on Valentine's Day 1981, it became one of the many victims of the severe recession in the paper industry at that time and was permanently closed down.

* * *

In 1770 James Moir, supported by a number of Aberdonians, set up a mill at

Stoneywood on the river Don – the estate of which he was owner. By 1771 sole control of the mill was in the hands of Alexander Smith who was joined in the venture by his son-in-law Patrick Pirie. For the next twenty years or so brown papers were produced.

Patrick Pirie died in 1787 and Alexander Smith in 1796. Smith had a son who died, aged 13, in 1800 so that the business passed to the grandson Alexander Pirie, one of the most famous names in the paper industry. Alex Pirie developed the mill over the next fifty years with his principal lieutenant James Reid. Between them they introduced white papers made from bleached rags, watermarking and, in 1820, commenced continuous production on the newly invented Fourdrinier papermachine.

Alex had four sons: Patrick, Francis, Alexander and Gordon. As we have seen Patrick, the eldest, opted for the cloth industry and was established at Gordon's Mills in which his father had a substantial interest. Although the other three sons were all involved at Stoneywood the most important contribution was made by Alex jnr. who guided the affairs of the company from 1840 until his death in 1875.

A limited company was formed in 1882, the shares of which were held by the Pirie family. The mill continued to expand the volume and diversity of its high-quality products. A total of nine papermachines was installed of which five are still in operation producing over 65,000 tonnes annually.

In 1922 the company amalgamated with Wiggins Teape & Co. and has recently joined forces with the French papermaker Arjomari and Appleton Paper of the USA to form the Arjo WT Appleton group.

* * *

Charles Smith, a nephew of the Alexander Smith of Stoneywood, went into partnership to produce paper with Charles Davidson of Bucksburn, the millwright son of a local farming family. When Alexander Smith died in 1796 the partnership was dissolved and Charles Davidson began to operate the paper mill by himself. The mill was located about half a mile downstream of Stoneywood on the Don at a site known as Mugiemoss.

In 1830 William and George Davidson entered the business. George sold his share and William continued alone until, in turn, his five sons were introduced. Brown papers were made, principally for bags and wrappings. One of the sons, George jnr. invented a bag making machine which revolutionised the bag trade where, previously, bags had been made by hand. The paper mill expanded to manufacture the paper for the growing business obtained by the bag factory. Later, felt paper for carpet underlays was developed. In the 1920s and until the mid-1930s competition from foreign imports was extreme. In 1936 the company diversified into multi-ply board manufacture using collected wastepaper as the fibre source.

In 1953 the company, C. Davidson & Sons, was acquired by British Plaster

Mugiemoss Paper Mills, owned by Charles Davidson & Sons Ltd.

Board Ltd, but retained its name. In 1965 a new multi-ply Inverform board machine was installed to produce the board which forms the surface liner of plaster board which is used extensively in the building trade. The papermaking operation was later closed leaving two board machines now extensively modernised and producing over 200,000 tonnes annually using wastepaper as the fibrous raw material.

* * *

The Tait family were large landowners having settled over 300 years ago near Inverurie, some 17 miles from Aberdeen. Their land was bounded to the north-east by the river Don. Their early interests included granite quarrying as well as grain milling. They helped to finance a canal between Inverurie and Aberdeen which was opened in 1807. In the mid-nineteenth century the railway to Inverurie was built and cut across their land. The canal was closed, as a result of which they received some financial compensation from the railway company who wished to eliminate competition. In 1860 the family started a paper mill beside the river.

In the 1860s the use of esparto grass from the Mediterranean countries had been developed as a papermaking fibre. Taits set up grass boiling and washing equipment and based their manufacture on esparto. Printing and writing papers and boards were produced. Problems with river pollution

Aberdeen, Merket Cross and Union Street, c. 1890. Town House is the tallest building in the background.

from the effluent generated from grass boiling eventually led to a change to chemical woodpulp. Two small papermachines were operated until the late 1960s when a new machine was ordered from Bertrams of Edinburgh.

In 1986 a large twin-wire high-speed machine was purchased from Voith of West Germany. By this time the original two machines had been shut down. The mill, which was family owned through five generations until 1989, was acquired by the Federal Paper Company of New Jersey, USA, and is now known as Federal Tait. The two machines in present operation produce approximately 200,000 tonnes of printings and writings in reels and cut sheets.

* * *

In the late nineteenth century the last of the five papermills was established. The formation of Gordon's Mills Paper Company was announced in 1888. The Company lasted only two or three years and then ceased operation. In 1893 the mill, with all equipment, was purchased from the liquidator and the Donside Paper Company was formed.

CHAPTER FOUR

The Early Days of The Donside Paper Company

AN ANNOUNCEMENT OF an addition to the Aberdeen Paper Industry was made in the *Aberdeen Journal* of 16 January 1888. Quoting from the newspaper article:

> Among the various industries for which Aberdeen is famed the manufacture of paper certainly takes a prominent place. The annual output of the extensive mills along the lower reaches of the Don, as also from the works at Peterculter, is enormous. In spite of the prevailing depression the paper manufacturing companies around Aberdeen are still able to hold their own and to pay substantial dividends. As there is every reason to believe that this industry is capable of still further expansion locally a company has been formed for the purpose of carrying on the business of manufacturing and trading in paper at Gordon's Mills.

The chairman of the new company – Gordon's Mills Paper Co. – was a Mr

James H. Bower. He was also a director of Culter Mills Paper Co. demonstrating that even in those days the Aberdeen paper industry was a close-knit affair. The manager of the new mill was Mr Shand who was quoted as having a 'large experience of papermaking' gained apparently in India. He entered into the company with 'great zeal and enterprise'.

The capital of the new company was £50,000 in 10,000 shares of £5 each, the first issue of which was £30,000. Local interest from the prominent citizens of the day was brisk and the first issue was quickly absorbed. The unexpired lease (42 years) of the property was purchased from the trustees of the late Mr Mess who had operated the meal mill. The company intended to produce 'middles for cardboard makers, railway tickets, casings, manillas, cutlery papers (glazed and unglazed), also all kinds of grocery papers such as wrappings and bags in all colours glazed and unglazed'.

The papermachine of 98-inches width was one of the widest in Scotland and was powered by a new steam-engine of 390 hp. A new coal-fired boiler plant was installed, coal at that time costing between 12s. and 17s. (60p to 85p) per ton. One of the existing waterwheels, '20 feet in diameter and 16 feet wide', powered by the flow in the mill lade was used to drive other equipment. The main production building consisted of four storeys, the process starting on the top floor and finished paper emerging at ground level. It was stated that 'all the latest improvements which science has devised will be introduced into the mechanical department'. No difficulty in obtaining 'a sufficient number of skilled and experienced workers' was anticipated, indeed it was stated that 'this enterprise will undoubtedly prove a boon to the industrial classes of Woodside'.

Signatures of the original shareholders, 11 July 1893.

V.—The Capital of the Company is £25,000, divided into 5,000 Shares of £5 each, with power to increase or reduce the Capital, and to issue any of the Shares of original Capital or Shares of increased Capital as Preferential, Guaranteed, or Deferred Shares, and to consolidate or subdivide the Shares of the Company.

We, the several persons whose names and addresses are subscribed, are desirous of being formed into a Company, in pursuance of this Memorandum of Association, and we respectively agree to take the number of shares in the Capital of the Company set opposite our respective names.

Names and Addresses of Subscribers.	Number of Shares taken by each Subscriber.
[illegible]	One share
Wm C Leng, Newspaper Proprietor [illegible] Dundee	One Share
C. M. Pattullo [illegible]	One Share
Catherine [illegible] Cupar Fife spinster	One Share
[illegible] Printing Manager, Bank Street, Dundee	One Share
William [illegible] 11 Reform St. Dundee	One share
Henry C. Pattullo, Solicitor, Bank St Dundee	One share

Dated this Eleventh day of July, Eighteen hundred and ninety-three.

Witness to the above Signatures,

John [illegible] 1 Bank Street, Dundee, Law Clerk.

All appeared set for success of the new venture yet sad to relate it lasted for only two or three years. Just why it failed is not known but the continuing recession, the very wide grade range, poor prices and foreign competition – all very real problems for the papermakers of the time – probably combined to snuff out the new mill almost at birth.

On 14 and 15 June 1893 Sir John Leng of Kinbrae, Newport-on-Tay, an MP for Dundee, and James Pattullo, a solicitor from Ashmore, near Blairgowrie, Perthshire, signed a Memorandum of Agreement to purchase the mill, machinery and leases from the Official Liquidator. The agreed price was £11,000. The Donside Paper Company was formed by Memorandum of Association on 11 July 1893. It was a private Limited Company with seven equal shareholders none of whom came from Aberdeen. One of the first objects of the new company was to 'purchase and acquire the leasehold property known as Gordon's Mills from Sir John Leng and James Pattullo'. The authorised capital of the Company was £25,000 in 5,000 shares of £5 of which £16,000 was issued initially. The registered office was 1 Bank Street, Dundee.

Sir John Leng became the first Chairman of the company. Apart from his political activities he had interests in the jute industry and newspaper publishing in Dundee.

The other shareholders were:

James Pattullo	Solicitor, Blairgowrie
William C. Leng (Sir John's son)	Newspaper proprietor, Dundee
Charles M. Pattullo	Papermaker, Dundee
Catherine Westwood	Spinster, Cupar, Fife
Alex Banks	Printing manager, Dundee
William Low	Advertising manager, Dundee
Henry A. Pattullo	Solicitor, Dundee (also Company Secretary)

Map, c. 1900, showing the position of Donside Paper Mills in the Gordon's Mills site. The woollen mills and Don Cottage can be seen above.

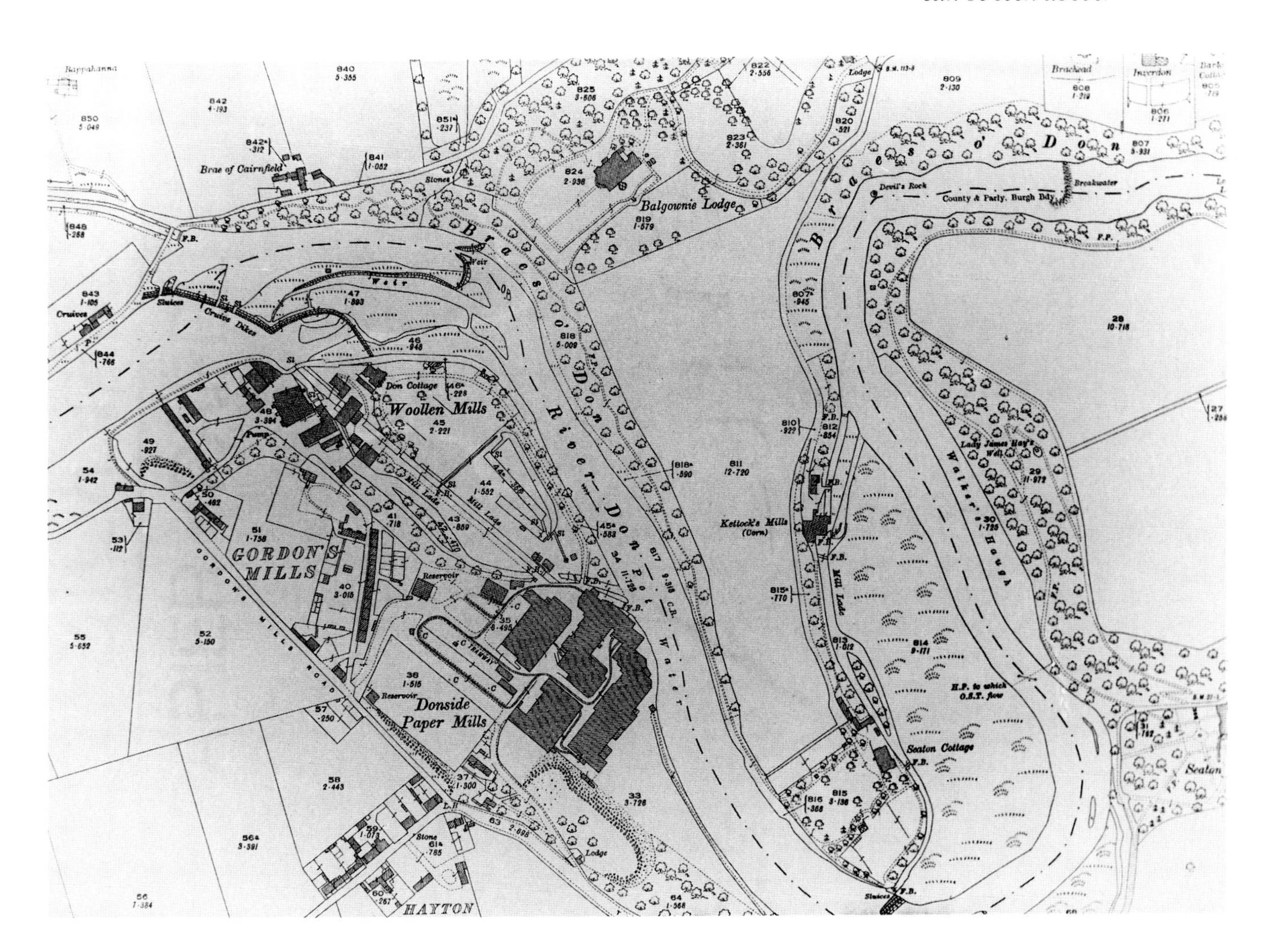

The Leng family newspaper interests were closely associated and later merged with those of D. C. Thomson, to this day a famed and fiercely independent publisher of regional newspapers, periodicals and annuals with whom Donside still maintains a close business relationship.

At the time the investment in papermaking by the shareholders represented an early example of vertical integration with a local source of supply. Charles Pattullo managed the mill and commanded a salary of £5.00 per week. He was also entitled to an annual bonus which was geared to the percentage by which the declared dividend exceeded 5 per cent, thus demonstrating that performance-related pay is no new phenomenon.

The company operated one machine which was dedicated to the manufacture of newsprint and related products such as mechanical printings mostly sold in reels thus reducing mill processing costs and wastage from paper cutting operations. Weekly output was 50 tons. With a narrow product range the first year of operation yielded a profit of £2,267, a handsome return on the capital investment. The dividend declared was 5 per cent. Wages paid were £1,945 and salaries £408 – Sir John certainly ran a tight ship!

The mill prospered through the early years of the twentieth century, a period of greater profitability than papermakers had enjoyed for a long time, despite growing foreign competition and increasing costs. Total annual output of paper production in the UK passed one million tons for the first time.

Locally, increasing industrialisation beside the Don was causing concern to the fishing proprietors on the lower reaches. In October 1893 the local press carried a report of a meeting of the Don Salmon Fishery Board at which the adverse effect of increased pollution on the fishings was discussed. A direct complaint against Donside Paper Co. was lodged by the Fishery Board in a letter to the Aberdeen City Council in February 1898. In this letter it was alleged that 'Donside Paper Company are causing to fall or flow or knowingly permitting to fall or flow or be carried into the river Don poisonous, noxious or polluting liquid whereby offences are being committed'. The letter went on to ask the Council to take steps for the removal of said cause of pollution and incidentally to deal with discharges of domestic sewage.

At the time the Council was designing the Northern Trunk Sewer and negotiations of wayleaves were, as always, a difficult hurdle to surmount. Various entries in the Council minutes in the next few years are to be found on this subject relating to the immediate vicinity of the mill. The solution finally agreed was that, in exchange for a number of wayleaves to allow sewer pipes to cross land belonging to Donside, the mill was granted permission to discharge effluent into the northern sewer. Since the sewer discharged direct to the North Sea from an outfall beyond Aberdeen harbour none of the mill's effluent was returned to the Don. This arrangement, which is still in effect, produced a permanent solution to the river pollution problem which has

Paper winder, with super calender to the right.

caused difficulty and great expense for the other paper mills on the Don.

At an Extraordinary General Meeting of the Company on 6 December 1911, by special resolution, Donside became a public company and the mill became the registered office which it has remained to the present time. The 5,000 existing £5 shares were substituted with 25,000 £1 shares. Shortly after this Frederick Becker became Chairman. He had started in business as a woodpulp and paper merchant after which he expanded into paper manufacture forming the Marsden Group of companies, in which there were twelve mills, mostly in Yorkshire. His other business interests included a shipping company. He clearly liked the Aberdeen area because he took up residence and later purchased Don Cottage, the owner's house which had been built on Gordon's Mills site many years previously. Subsequently, after he had been knighted, he moved to Ellon Castle, 17 miles north of Aberdeen.

Shortly after Donside became a public company the capital structure was increased by an issue of debentures. This was used to finance a substantial increase in newsprint production at the mill. Two new, high speed, modern machines were ordered from Charles Walmsley of Bury, Lancs. The first which cost £22,500 (including the building) was commissioned in January 1914 but the second did not start until after the end of the First World War. They were the fastest-running newsprint machines in Britain, running at 600 feet/minute and with a combined output of 400 tons per week.

Special resolution to convert Donside Paper to a public company, 6 December 1911.

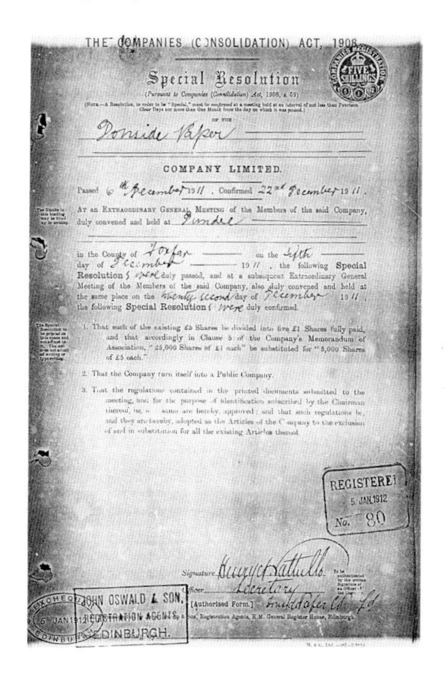

THE COMPANIES (CONSOLIDATION) ACT, 1908.

Special Resolution

(Pursuant to Companies (Consolidation) Act, 1908, s. 69)

OF THE

Donside Paper

COMPANY LIMITED.

Passed 6th December 1911. Confirmed 22nd December 1911.

At an Extraordinary General Meeting of the Members of the said Company, duly convened and held at Dundee in the County of Forfar on the fifth day of December 1911, the following Special Resolutions were duly passed, and at a subsequent Extraordinary General Meeting of the Members of the said Company, also duly convened and held at the same place on the twenty second day of December 1911, the following Special Resolutions were duly confirmed.

1. That each of the existing £5 Shares be divided into five £1 Shares fully paid, and that accordingly in Clause 5 of the Company's Memorandum of Association, "25,000 Shares of £1 each" be substituted for "5,000 Shares of £5 each."
2. That the Company turn itself into a Public Company.
3. That the regulations contained in the printed documents submitted to the meeting, and for the purpose of identification subscribed by the Chairman thereof, be, and the same are hereby, approved; and that such regulations be, and they are hereby, adopted as the Articles of the Company to the exclusion of and in substitution for all the existing Articles thereof.

REGISTERED 5 JAN 1912 No. 80

Signature Henry C. Nattiello

Officer Secretary

[Authorised Form.] Donside Paper Co. Ltd

JOHN OSWALD & SON, REGISTRATION AGENTS, EDINBURGH.

Donside steam lorry at Aberdeen Harbour collecting wood pulp, c. 1920. The lorry was used for journeys as far as Perth, eighty miles away.

During the war newspapers and cheap printing papers were in great demand. Mr Becker, with his knowledge of the pulp market and the many contacts he had in that business, was able to ensure adequate supplies for the mill. Good profits were made although the government took the cream off that situation when it introduced Excess Profits Duty of 66⅔ per cent on a retrospective basis to the beginning of the war!

At the end of the war Major W. Geoffrey Moore, who was Mr Becker's son-in-law, joined the Company and later became Managing Director. In the aftermath of the war a short inflationary boom developed and 1919 and 1920 were very good years where wartime import restrictions were maintained thus affording some protection for home manufacturers. The mill also built an export trade with British colonies, periodically shipping 1,500-ton consignments to the Antipodes from Aberdeen. Successful issues of ordinary shares and debentures were made at this time. In the prospectus for the debenture issue Mr Becker referred to the ability of the Company to sustain ordinary dividend payments of 10 per cent in previous years.

These good times came to an abrupt end and a slump ensued. Papermakers were caught in a situation where they were still paying for raw materials at the prices prevailing in the boom period while their selling prices had collapsed. It was described as 'the worst patch papermakers had encountered'.

At Donside, which had three machines in production, unsold stocks built up until there was over three months supply of newsprint in store at the mill. In this period many mills closed down and half the industry workforce were either on short time or out of work. Mills began to join forces to form larger groups. It was during this period that Alex Pirie & Co. of Stoneywood joined Wiggins Teape. The Inveresk Paper Group, which had developed from the single mill near Musselburgh, had enlarged considerably through the amalgamation of a number of family-owned mills mainly in the central belt of Scotland.

Donside continued under the Chairmanship of Sir Frederick Becker who had been knighted in 1922. This event was noted by a 'Programme of

Beater house for stock preparation; pulp bales around beaters. J. Edmonds stands on the right. The Edmonds family has a long and continuing history of service in the Mill.

Scenes from the 1920s. Right: *Wire baling.* Below: *No. 1 paper-machine – wet end – with drive pulleys above and behind, c. 1927.*

4. When all is said and done you are not giving much and you are to-day undeniably well off compared to others—why make yourselves less well-off?

To return to sentiment, it is the subscriber's sincere wish to point out in a perfectly friendly and frank way that you have nothing to gain and everything to lose. This is not meant at all as a threat but my heart grieves for the unfortunate, misled employees of a mill that has taken this ill chosen moment to quarrel with their bread and cheese. Only those affected or in close contact with it can realise the misery and suffering to families caused by unemployment. For goodness sake don't put yourself in that position—don't even jeopardise that wonderful relationship that exists at Donside between employer and employee, a relationship of which both are, I know, proud.

If you are so determined that you want to change the order of things, wait until Sir Frederick comes up to Don. He will at least try to understand your point of view, but he wont if you hold a pistol at his head by the sudden drastic action I understand you contemplate.

We would like it quite plainly understood that we are not making money by the 144 hour week, but we are avoiding greater loss in the hope that by keeping the mill running we will be in the position of making money when the trade revival comes along. If we are compelled to shut now it will be a long time before we are in the running again with other mills that do keep going.

I should be very pleased to meet any committee of men who would like to discuss the matter further.

W. G. MOORE,
Major.

Letter from the Managing Director Geoffrey Moore to the work force which attempts to discourage industrial action, 1922.

Entertainment to Employees' held at Ellon Castle in September of the same year. A special train from Aberdeen was run and there was a procession from Ellon station to the castle. Sports events, a five-a-side football competition and a dance programme were the main features of the day. The Becker's son-in-law was on the organising committee and revealed his military background by arranging for a bugle to be sounded to summon the assembled company to Dinner and Tea!

Business conditions in the next few years became very tough with profitability on newsprint barely above break-even level. The company ran into serious debt and the situation was not helped when a number of their external investments failed. By late 1923 the directors of Donside were carrying on the business under the supervision of a committee of creditors. In March 1924 the company petitioned the Lords of Session to sanction a scheme of arrangement by which the company would settle with its main creditors (three banks) in exchange for a further issue of debentures. The only other alternative was liquidation! The proposal was approved and the Company continued trading but still in very difficult conditions.

Programme for the Summer Outing to Ellon Castle, 1922. Entertainment included field sports and dancing.

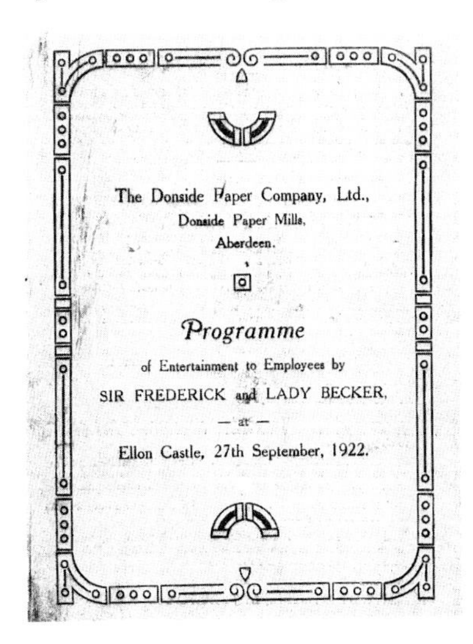
The Donside Paper Company, Ltd.,
Donside Paper Mills,
Aberdeen.

Programme
of Entertainment to Employees by
SIR FREDERICK and LADY BECKER,
— at —
Ellon Castle, 27th September, 1922.

Frederick Becker (centre) with 'strike breaking' staff and students during the 1926 General Strike.

An extract from the mill accounts for March 1925 reveals that the tonnage made in the month was 1,823, sales value £33,463, variable costs were £18,860 and fixed costs took nearly all of the remainder leaving a mere £278 of profit or just over half-a-crown a ton on paper sold! The situation was precarious and action was needed to reduce the burden of fixed costs. The time had come to consider amalgamation with a group so that management and selling expenses would be spread over a number of mills within the group.

By 1927 the Inveresk Paper Company, which had been acquiring shares in Donside during this period, owned nearly 80 per cent of the equity. Although Donside continued to operate as a separate company it became, effectively, part of the Inveresk Group.

CHAPTER FIVE

The Inveresk Years

Graveyard, St Machar's Cathedral

BY 1927 THE Inveresk Paper Group had become the largest paper producer in Scotland. It consisted of seven mills located mainly in the Forth and Clyde valleys manufacturing a wide range of paper and ɔard including coated papers. The Group Chairman was William Harrison ıo was also chairman of a number of other limited companies in the UK.
When Donside was absorbed into the group it continued as a public npany with the head office at the mill; thus it retained a separate identity. ɜw Board of Directors was appointed. William Harrison became ırman and three directors of other Inveresk mills, at Carrongrove, ·keithing and Glossop, were voted on to the board. The connection with ing was maintained through another director who was also on the l of Odham's Press. After the take-over Sir Frederick Becker's son-in-law ·rey Moore retained his position as Managing Director of Donside Paper ›any. Shortly before Sir Frederick died in 1935 Major Moore left and ! Clyde Paper Co., a newsprint mill in Glasgow.
manufacture of newsprint in standard grades and substances and s (machine and supercalendered) as well as mechanical printings ıed to be the principal output from the two papermachines. The l 98-in. machine was dismantled and reinstalled at the Inveresk mill at ·ithing. Capital expenditure was very limited in the years preceding

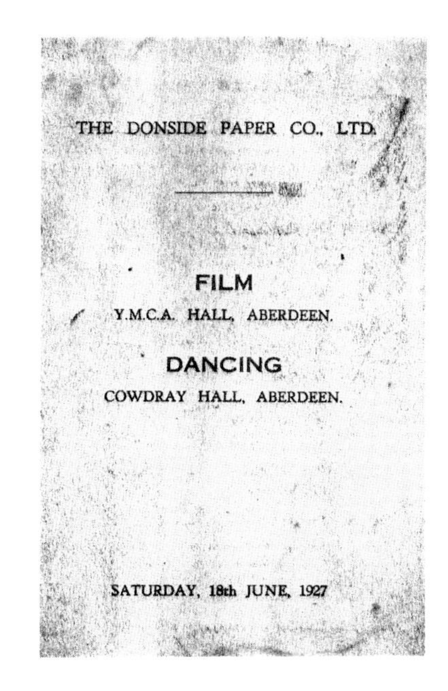

THE DONSIDE PAPER CO., LTD.

FILM

Y.M.C.A. HALL, ABERDEEN.

DANCING

COWDRAY HALL, ABERDEEN.

SATURDAY, 18th JUNE, 1927

Geoffrey Moore, Sir Frederick Beckers' son-in-law and Managing Director, c. *1928.*

and immediately following the Second World War. Since the production was mainly sold as reels only rudimentary cutting and other finishing equipment were required. The supercalenders, used to improve the paper surface smoothness, operated at only modest line pressure and were quite basic in design.

Consumption of newsprint in Britain had burgeoned and domestic mills with narrow, slower machines could not keep up with demand. By the start of the Second World War in 1939 at least half of the newsprint required was imported, mainly from Canada and Scandinavia. Producers in these countries were often subsidised by their governments but, in the case of newsprint, neither restriction of import volume nor protection for home producers, by application of tariffs, was ever exercised by the UK government.

Within two months of the outbreak of war all pulp stocks were taken over by the Ministry of Supply which, using a licence system, allocated licences they considered appropriate to the war effort. Woodpulp continued to be imported despite the dangers to cargo vessels in the North Sea and Atlantic. Newsprint and mechanical printings continued to be in great demand although newspaper sheet size and substance were reduced. Shortages of dyes, rosin, china clay and other chemicals affected the quality and brightness of papers produced. Another profound change that occurred was the employment of large numbers of women to perform tasks which had hitherto been the exclusive province of men.

Recovery after the war was a slow process. This was compounded by the continuation of the wartime licence system for purchases of woodpulp. As late as 1951 The Paper Controller cut the allocation of pulp by 20 per cent. In 1952 the Donside Board noted that profitability was very poor because pulp licences were granted specifically for the manufacture of paper for government use and abysmally low selling prices were obtained from HM Stationery Office.

However the real problem confronting Donside was the serious lack of competitiveness of the mill's two small machines compared with the much larger and faster machines then being installed elsewhere in the UK and abroad. The crunch came when Bowaters installed four new newsprint machines and Reeds two in the 1950s. Each of these machines was three times faster and more than twice the width of the Donside machines which were rendered obsolete for making newsprint economically. If the mill was

Paper cutter with crew.

Paper inspection and packing in the Salle, 1940s.

to survive it was essential that production was switched to higher-quality grades which would command a better price per ton. By the late 1940s it had been decided to make a phased move to 'woodfree' plain and machine-coated grades.

In order to fulfil the market requirements for the new grades a programme of capital expenditure was authorised. This included new stock-preparation plant including refiners, additional and replacement power plant and cutters, guillotines and ancillary equipment required for selling the mill output in sheets cut to customer-specified sizes. The papermachines were equipped with size presses and Champion metering bar coaters installed in the drying section of the machines. Since it was possible to bypass these coating stations the machines were able to make coated or uncoated woodfree papers with an all chemical pulp furnish. Also there was still a contractual requirement to supply some newsprint to various Scottish newspapers such as the *Edinburgh Evening News*, *Glasgow Herald* and the Dundee papers.

For a few years the mill produced the new grades side by side with newsprint until production of the latter finally ceased in 1955. An executive of the local newspaper, the *Press and Journal*, was later to remark that 'it was a pity that Donside no longer makes newsprint because, although we did not place our main order with them, it was so handy to be able to lift the

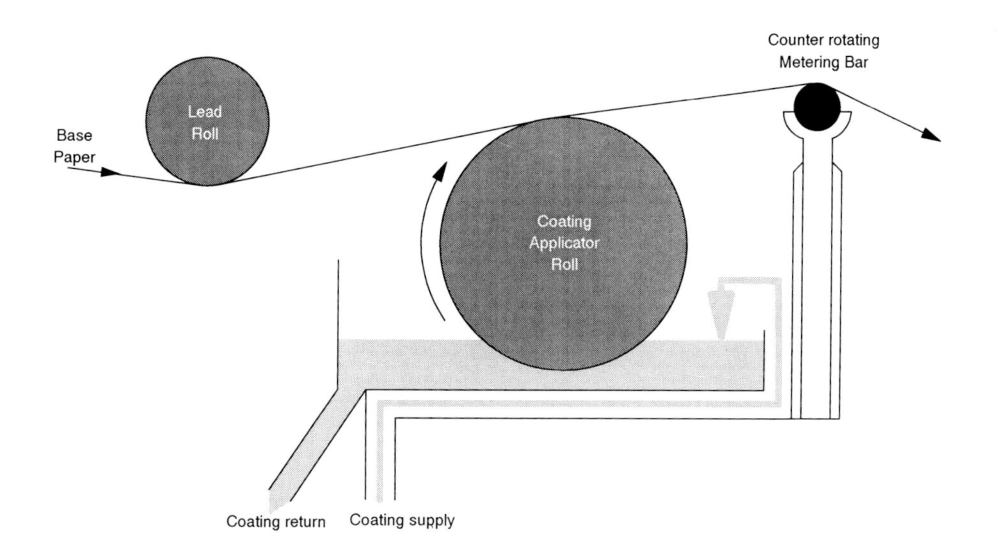

Principle of champion metering bar coating.

phone and order another reel or two for immediate delivery if we were short on a Saturday night print-run.'

Application of a fine china clay/latex coating to the sized surfaces of the sheet followed by off-machine supercalendering produced glossy paper suitable for medium-quality printing in monochrome or colour. Paper produced by the mill was used for mail order catalogues, travel brochures, colour magazines, periodicals and labels of the time. The brand names of the coated papers were Don Art for the woodfree coated range and Thistlecote for the coated mechanicals.

The manufacture of higher-quality papers required significant changes to be made. Improved standards of sheet cleanliness, uniformity and printability were essential. Development of coating mixes appropriate to the eventual printing technique received continuous attention. More quality control and mill testing was introduced to monitor production through the increased number of processes involved.

A new department was formed for the specific purpose of cutting and guillotining paper to required sizes, inspection of each group of cut sheets, wrapping of individual reams and stacking for delivery on wooden pallets. These conversion processes were labour-intensive and a far cry from the practice of simply despatching wrapped reels of newsprint to customers.

Retained earnings for the previous years when Donside was making newsprint were insufficient to finance these developments. Therefore Inveresk Group provided a series of cash advances (totalling £400,000) to the mill, further increasing its dependence on the Group. In 1959, at an Extraordinary General Meeting of the Company, it was resolved that the

Company be converted into a private company again with Inveresk as the only shareholder. There followed a period where profits were somewhat more healthy at £80,000–£100,000 per year compared with the previous near break-even situation. The long-term future of the mill was still uncertain however.

Standards of printing and new techniques were advancing rapidly and with them the demands on paper, in particular coated grades, became more and more stringent. The Champion metering bar coaters at Donside were capable of applying only 10–11 grams per sq. metre of coating per side of the sheet and this was insufficient to provide the surface for higher-quality work. Higher speeds of printing machines required improved paper runnability with minimal defects. Again the on-machine coaters proved inadequate to meet these criteria. Output rate and papermachine efficiency were both inhibited by the on-machine coating process and this, in turn, limited the mill's profit potential.

In 1961 Blandin Paper Company in Wisconsin, USA, had developed a new coating machine. It operated separately from the papermachine and was referred to as an off-machine trailing blade coater. A thin layer of coating was applied to the full width of each paper surface in turn by means of a stiff steel blade held against the paper under controlled pressure. During this operation support for the paper was provided by a hard rubber covered backing roll. By adjustment of the pressure and angle at which the blade was applied and the use of appropriate coating formulations it proved possible to apply much greater coat weight with more even distribution than with any other coating technique.

Many paper companies worldwide were installing trailing blade coaters to increase output and quality. In 1964 the Inveresk Group Board took the bold decision to enter this new field and embarked on the largest capital expenditure programme it had ever undertaken. Donside was the group mill chosen for this investment.

At this time, before the development of the recently discovered North Sea oil which brought wealth to the region, Aberdeen and the north-east of Scotland was an area which qualified for Regional Development Grants from central government. Since the new project would create additional jobs at all levels it also attracted local employment grants. These factors helped to tip the scales in favour of Donside when Inveresk Group were considering the location for the investment.

This project improved every aspect of mill operation. A new oil-fired boiler and associated turbo-alternator replaced the existing power plant. A fully instrumented continuous stock preparation plant with additional pulp refiners was installed to supply the papermachines. The older of the two papermachines was scrapped and replaced with a brand new machine while the other machine was extensively refurbished.

Following the papermachines, two paper inspection winders were installed to prepare paper reels for off-machine coating. A trailing blade coater of the most modern design was installed in a new building constructed specifically for the purpose of paper coating and finishing. The new paper-finishing equipment comprised two high-speed paper winders and a supercalender capable of exerting greater line pressure for improving coated paper smoothness and gloss.

A new, automated coating preparation plant was designed and constructed. In the paper conversion and sheeting department a new high-capacity multi-reel paper cutter with statistical sampling capability was installed on the floor of the new conversion building above the blade coater.

When the installation was completed the capacity of the mill was expected to reach 46,000 tons per year which was more than double the previous output.

The centrepiece of the whole installation was the Highland Chief as the blade coater was named. The success and future profitability of not only Donside but the Inveresk Group depended heavily on the performance of the new technology. Additional senior staff were appointed to strengthen the production, laboratory and engineering departments. A 'know-how' agreement was signed with the Oxford Paper Company of Maine, USA, by

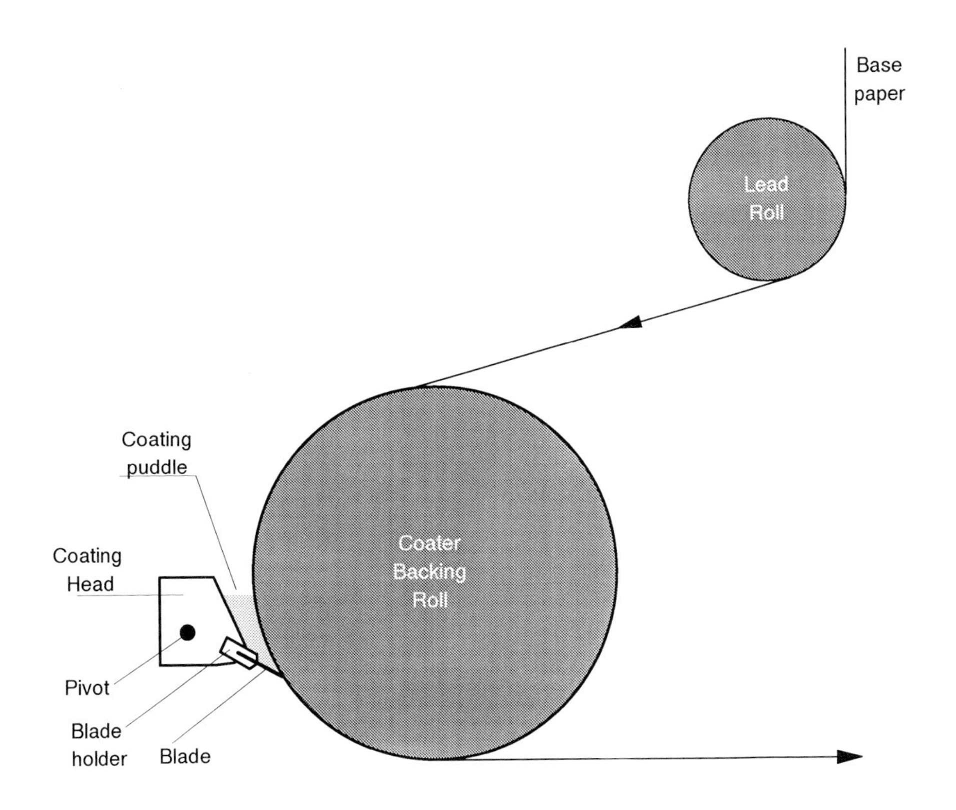

Principle of blade coating.

Princess Alexandra at the formal start-up of the Highland Chief, 1967.

which Inveresk purchased information regarding coating-formulation recipes and base paper specifications. New coated grades were designed to meet the requirements of the printing processes. These carried the brand name Clan which identified the Inveresk Group products. Technical and production personnel from the two companies exchanged visits and crew training for key production personnel was arranged at the Oxford Mill in Rumford, Maine. The expressed intention was to make Donside 'one of the most modern coating mills in the whole of Europe'.

The work, arranged in phases to minimise loss of output, was completed in 1967 and to celebrate the completion of the project Princess Alexandra was invited to perform the official opening of what was, essentially, a new mill. The opening took place on 15 September 1967 and was attended by the Princess and her husband, the Lord Provost of Aberdeen, the Chairman of Inveresk Group, the Managing Director and their wives together with 300 other guests.

Everything seemed to be in place. Production started with the future of both Donside and Inveresk heavily dependent on the success and profitability of the venture. Fifteen months later these high hopes had been dashed, the mill was generating very heavy losses and teetering on the brink of closure, the Group's finances were in disarray and their bankers were demanding immediate action.

Facing page: *View of Donside Mill from downstream.*

CHAPTER SIX

The Albatross

81 High Street, Old Aberdeen

TO UNDERSTAND WHAT went wrong requires an appreciation of the essentials of off-machine blade-coating. This production technique was firmly established by the late 1960s and blade-coated papers became the printers' first choice. They were able to produce better, more consistent printed results and operating performance was better on printing-machines of all types. By the nature of its design the blade coater eliminated many paper faults which previously, if unnoticed in inspection and passed to the printer, caused downtime, spoilage and printing plate damage. For these reasons the blade coater earned the justified nickname of 'the printer's friend'.

Successful blade coating requires very high standards of base-papermaking and cleanliness. The coater runs faster than the papermachine (or machines) from which it is supplied with sized base paper. It must run continuously which means that, as one reel of base paper expires, the start of a new reel must be spliced at speed to the last plies of the preceding reel. This operation, called 'flying splicing', performed at speeds exceeding 2,000 feet per minute, requires very careful design of the splice form and adhesive material used. Speeds of rotation of the two reels must be very carefully matched to avoid undue tension at the moment of splicing or the formation of an unwanted paper loop both of which lead to paper breaks.

The coating method, using steel blades, and the operating speed together provide a severe examination of base-paper quality and runnability. Any weakness leads to paper breaks within the coater with the resulting necessity of a lengthy shut-down to clean the coater, refeed the paper and regain previous coating and drying conditions.

Production losses at this stage are extremely expensive and poor running can adversely affect quality in the subsequent processes such as supercalendering, winding and cutting. Since blade coating and finishing are separate processes following papermaking, extended delays can occur between making the base paper and quality assessment of the final product. This could result in large quantities of part-finished paper already in process before the discovery of a defect which might render it unsuitable for the intended grade or customer.

In the normal process an allowance is made for wastage from edge-trimming, preparing reels for further processing and the like. A standard percentage is allowed and additional paper to cover these losses is made. If losses exceed the standard a shortfall will occur requiring the remake of part of the order. Remakes can play havoc with production planning, delivery schedules and papermachine and coater efficiency.

Every paper producer who had converted to blade coating experienced the problems of base-paper quality and runnability described and Donside was no exception. However Donside's learning curve was longer than most because their 'know how' agreement involved North American base-paper specifications, coating techniques and formulations. Unfortunately European requirements for surface smoothness and gloss of coated paper were higher than in the USA. As a result the standard of paper produced at Donside did not meet the domestic market requirement. Although the mill had employed new people with undoubted talent their experience of blade coating was minimal at the time. Lines of communication between Donside and Oxford Paper Company in the USA were long and inevitably delays in interpretation and action occurred.

Shortcomings also arose from the layout of equipment in the new finishing building. This created bottlenecks and production delays. Paper handling between the various off-machine processes proved slow, labour intensive and very costly. The area for cutting was situated on a floor 50 feet above the coater/finishing house and access for paper was by lift only. Ironically the despatch department was situated at ground-floor level which meant that all cut paper then took the reverse journey, again by lift.

Not surprisingly output was disappointing and barely reached 20,000 tons annually. In a desperate effort to boost production the papermachine speeds were increased but this had an adverse affect on base-paper quality which was reflected in poor runnability on the blade coater. The frequency of remakes fragmented the planned production schedules. Finished paper was

Don Cottage on the Old Gordon's Mills site was built as a mill owner's house.

often downgraded into sub-standard qualities and, as a result, offered to merchants specialising in the disposal of material of this type with a corresponding price penalty for the mill. Such was the aggregation of sub-standard paper that the mill storage areas became choked and an off-site warehouse was rented to accommodate it. This store was called 'The Mastrick Store'.

The new cutter was designed with a facility for discharging a selected percentage of cut sheets into a sampling bin. A statistical analysis of the sample was then carried out to determine the overall quality of the paper. The defects identified when inspecting the samples were such that almost all cut paper required subsequent manual inspection. This additional procedure entailed the employment of over 100 women which increased the process costs significantly and swelled the total number employed to 629.

Facing page: *Pulp bales stored ready for use, viewed across the settling pond.*

Through 1968 the mill operation was characterised by increasingly heavy financial losses. These reached a point where the losses made at Donside virtually eliminated all of the profits made in the remainder of the Inveresk Group mills. Referring to the Group report for 1968 the Group loss was £800,000. In the same year Donside made a loss of £988,000 on a turnover of just under £4,000,000 – a situation which would ruin any company. The Group bankers were extremely concerned that, if the losses at Donside continued, they could jeopardise the whole of Inveresk. As a consequence they counselled that the Group should dispose of The Donside Paper Company or that, as an alternative, it should be shut down completely.

Responding to the bank demands Inveresk set about the disposal of its prized asset. In late 1968 they approached their chief competitor in the UK, the Bowater Corporation which operated a successful blade-coating mill making woodfree grades at Sittingbourne in Kent. Donside was also offered to Reed International which had an off-machine blade coater making light-weight mechanical coated grades at Imperial Paper Mill in Gravesend, Kent. Both of these corporations declined to make any offer, arguing that the mill in Aberdeen was too remote from their own coating operations in the south of England.

At the time the government of the day had set up the Industrial Reorganisation Corporation with the remit of regenerating industry particularly in the regions and Scotland. The IRC was instrumental in 'persuading' Reed and Bowater jointly to acquire and operate Donside. The purchase price of £2 million was financed by a deferred interest loan of half that amount to each partner. A waiver was given from the Monopolies Commission despite the dominant position the two companies would occupy in the UK coated paper market. In turn the partners were committed to provide investment and working capital as required.

Agreement was reached on these matters and the partnership of Reed and Bowater, called the Consortium, took over the mill in February 1969. Inveresk used the proceeds of the sale of Donside to repair their finances. The Group returned to modest profitability in the following year, due mainly to what one of their senior executives in referring to the enforced sale of the mill called 'the removal of an albatross from the Group's affairs'.

CHAPTER SEVEN

The Consortium

THE TWO PARTNERS concluded an agreement for operating Donside and to develop their future coating interests on a joint basis.

It was agreed that the Donside Paper Company would operate as a separate financial entity and that any profits or losses would be apportioned equally between the two partners. It was also specified that each partner would first optimise profit in their wholly owned coating mills in Kent – Bowater at Sittingbourne and Reed at Imperial Mill, Gravesend.

Bowater assumed responsibility for production and mill management while Reed co-ordinated selling and marketing on behalf of Donside. The coated-paper sales forces of each partner were to represent Donside which would not have its own selling organisation. The partners' sales companies would be remunerated in the form of commission payable by Donside. There was also provision for financial compensation for any orders transferred to Donside from the partners' mills for technical reasons.

The agreement provided each partner with equal representation on the Donside Board with the Chairmanship rotating annually between the partners. The new Board included three main Board Directors and a further two directors of subsidiary companies from each of the partners.

Wilfred Broad, Finance Director of Reed International, was the first Chairman. He was a small, round man whose quiet manner disguised an

A view of the north side of the Mill.

acid-sharp brain combined with great determination and shrewdness. His first task was to obtain working finance for the mill, not too easy given Donside's recent record. He visited the Edinburgh headquarters of the Scottish banks many of which declined any participation. Wilfred, when rebuffed, politely withdrew and proceeded to the next banker on his list. He progressed as far as the Bank of Scotland before securing their agreement to grant overdraft facilities of £750,000 and acceptance credits of £300,000 (these were used for pulp purchases). In return the two partners gave guarantees which underpinned the financial package in the event of failure of the venture.

The Donside Paper Company continued to operate as a private company with the partners as equal shareholders. All mill accounting and banking functions were kept separate from the partners' affairs. This provided the Donside Board and particularly the management team with a very clear view of its financial status.

Immediately following the take-over a key role was played by another member of the Board, A. P. (Tony) Gammie, Production Director of Bowater UK Paper Co., which was a subsidiary of the Corporation. Previously he had managed the Sittingbourne mill which made Bowater's coated papers. For six weeks he was resident in Aberdeen and ran the mill. In this he was aided by a team of papermaking, coating, finishing and conversion experts that he had drafted up from Sittingbourne on a temporary basis. It had been decided to abandon the 'Clan' range manufactured at Donside since this identified the mill with its previous owners. The woodfree coating grades made at Sittingbourne were substituted. These were also made available to the Inveresk sales force for a short period.

Much was changed in a very short time. Modifications, sometimes drastic, were made to base-paper and woodpulp specifications, coating formulations, finishing and cutting techniques and organisation. A large programme of capital expenditure to deal with production bottlenecks quickly received Board approval. Finishing equipment layout was fundamentally altered to improve process flow after the coater and reduce paper handling and congestion.

The speed of change took many in the mill by surprise – often there was no time for the niceties of debate. It was akin to a serious accident where the paramedics have to work fast to stabilise the patient who will otherwise die. In these circumstances some rough handling sometimes occurs.

One incident typifies the atmosphere at the time. A change in the paper-making conditions had been specified by one of the visiting experts. Under pressure of time he failed to notify the mill's day superintendent of the change. The latter, on returning from lunch, discovered what had happened and concluded that his services were no longer required. He was leaving the company for good when, fortunately, he was intercepted by the expert from whom he received an apology, an explanation and a fatherly chat. This defused the situation but the mill came close to losing a valued papermaking superintendent, his name Ian Lakin, a key player in our story.

After the six-week period Tony Gammie and his team withdrew and the new manager, John Fedo, arrived at the mill. He had spent six years at the Bowater Mersey newsprint mill site in Cheshire. There he had managed a subsidiary company before joining the paper mill. Previously he had worked at Imperial Paper Mills in Kent which had been acquired by Reeds in a take-over. He had no detailed knowledge of coated paper manufacture nor any connection with Sittingbourne Mill. In the handover period Tony Gammie and he visited the paper store at Mastrick. As part of the takeover agreement the Consortium had undertaken to sell the accumulated sub-standard paper on behalf of Inveresk. Viewing the very large assortment of grades and sizes Gammie turned to Fedo and said 'Once this lot is sold and the store emptied, if you fill it again I'll fire you!' This example of management by objectives was taken to heart and, when the Mastrick store was eventually emptied, the unexpired lease was terminated.

Reviewing the situation in the post-takeover situation John Fedo quickly realised that the success of the operation would depend on the speed with which the mill personnel, who were somewhat shellshocked, could consolidate and develop the newly introduced production techniques. He sensed a fierce pride in the mill at all levels and set about channelling this

John Fedo, General Manager, Donside Paper Company, with 'Barney' Bennett, of Sittingbourne Mill, immediately following the take-over, April 1969.

energy to profitable effect. Rebuilding confidence and self-sufficiency within the management team was his first priority.

Production quality rapidly improved and statistical sampling at the paper-cutting stage was reintroduced; thus the need to inspect all paper ceased. This led to a large reduction in the inspection workforce (mainly female) in this area. Other areas of overmanning were addressed with some redundancies at staff and senior management levels. A new, smaller and more tightly knit management team was formed with responsibilities clearly defined. There was no shortage of talented people at the mill and appointments from outside were unnecessary.

A notable inclusion in this team was Ian Lakin as Production Manager. He assumed responsibility for all papermaking, coating, finishing, the mill laboratory and quality control. John Fedo had learned of the earlier incident with the visiting expert and reasoned, correctly, that someone who showed such spirit in the uncertain take-over period would respond well to the challenge of a key position. It proved to be an appointment of crucial importance and long term benefit to the mill.

Another major appointment was that of Ken Nicholson who headed the cutting, conversion, packing, despatch, mill sales and production departments. In this role he was responsible for scheduling production on the papermachines in good time for the subsequent processing, packing and despatch to meet the delivery promises. Thanks to his energy this appointment was another success and Donside gained a high reputation for service.

Finance and mill administration at the time was the province of the Company Secretary, the late Gilbert Urquhart, a doughty Highland Scot if ever there was one! Bruce Stuart headed the engineering group which dealt with capital expenditure as well as mill maintenance. Alistair Dinnie, Personnel Manager, completed the top team. He was, and still is, highly respected in his twin role as 'father confessor' to the workforce and adviser and 'conscience' to the management team.

By the terms of the Consortium agreement Donside had no sales force. The company relied on orders generated by the partners' sales forces. A marketing co-ordinator was appointed to represent Donside interests in this vital area. However, since the mill was making only brands marketed by Bowater and Reed it could not relate directly to customers nor were its products branded with the Donside name. Furthermore the respective sales forces perceived that only half the profit from sales won for Donside accrued to their employer – not the greatest performance incentive for them.

In the Consortium agreement there was another provision which had a much more serious effect and, for the next eight years, inhibited the progress to profit-making and survival. As we shall see in the next chapter it had near fatal consequences for Donside.

CHAPTER EIGHT

Survival

AS NOTED EARLIER a fundamental principle of the Consortium agreement was that it should optimise profit at the partners' coating mills. Consequently Donside, in practice, operated initially as an overflow facility. It had no separate product range and no sales force of its own. Thus the order book relied on the Consortium's sales of coated paper being in excess of the production capacity of the partners' mills in Kent. In periods when sales were good the floodgates of mill activity would open. If a market downturn occurred then the overflow would reduce, sometimes drastically, and long spells of idle time were experienced in Aberdeen whilst the southern mills were relatively unaffected. In general, profitability at Donside was determined by these variations in activity. Export sales could raise production levels but, since these could be gained only at very low prices, it did not significantly improve profit.

The Consortium Board, having defined the operating conditions in their agreement, left matters to the Donside management team which reported back through Tony Gammie for a number of years. His other responsibilities widened, placing great pressures on his time. He was promoted to Chairman of Bowater UK Paper Company and then to the main Corporation Board before moving to North America to become Chief Executive Officer of Bowater Inc. The informal arrangement he agreed with the Donside manager was that 'If you need anything vital call me and if I want any information I will contact you.' As a consequence the Donside management team had a greater degree of self-determination than was usual for a relatively small subsidiary in a large organisation. They adopted a pragmatic approach, dealing with things as they were and not arguing how they might be in an ideal situation.

In matters of cash flow, financing capital expenditure and controlling the overdraft the mill looked straight down the barrel of the gun held by the Bank of Scotland in Market Street, Aberdeen. It is a tribute to the mill's accounting function that, at no time during the following nine years, was the agreed overdraft limit ever exceeded. Gilbert Urquhart summed up the position when he explained 'We all knew what the partners would say, and probably do, if the mill overstepped its financial limits. After all they had their money problems too.'

During the course of the 1970s the mill rode the 'boom and bust' economic conditions created by such factors as the miners' strike, the three-day week, the Prices and Incomes Board and the Six Day War with the after-effects of the latter quadrupling energy prices virtually overnight. In years when demand for coated paper was high the mill demonstrated its ability to make good profits. In one period of sustained high activity the overdraft was completely extinguished and a growing credit balance established. This impressive achievement was rewarded by the 'assistance' of the partners who each took an interest-free loan of £300,000 from the mill to ensure that the bank did not cancel the overdraft facility.

In the leaner times, with the papermachines either shut or on short-time working, rumours about the future of the mill were rife. On one occasion the phone rang in John Fedo's office and a voice enquired whether he could make an offer for the main turbo-alternator set. On being asked why he imagined it was for sale the reply was 'Well, the mill is closing down isn't it?' The record was set straight and the caller duly despatched. Rumours affected the attitude of major suppliers too. The company supplying heavy fuel oil for the main boiler plant insisted on payment of their monthly invoice within eighteen days. They always obtained payment because their representative 'camped' in the mill office foyer on the eighteenth day until he received the cheque. No cheque, no oil!

Periods of idle time were used to run development trials on the papermachines, coater and coating formulations. The mill was one of the first to manufacture base paper under alkaline conditions in the stock preparation and machine backwater systems. This superseded the previous method in which the addition of aluminium sulphate (alum) into the water system created highly acidic papermaking conditions. It was a notable achievement because both chemical and mechanical pulps, requiring differing chemical treatment, were used in the range of grades manufactured.

Base paper produced under alkaline conditions is stronger than that made using alum and the furnish cost is also reduced. Calcium carbonate is used as the sheet filler material, replacing china clay. The paper also lasts much longer – a feature which is essential for valuable printed material like fine books and documents where deterioration in storage can be disastrous. An alkaline system is compatible with a whole range of very fine coating materials such as ground or precipitated calcium carbonate, the use of which would not be possible in an acid paper machine water system. Later this factor became crucial when developing the higher-quality grades.

The Highland Chief, being of later design than the coaters in the southern mills, afforded opportunities for judicious modification and cost reduction of the coating formulations which were introduced after the take-over. It was essential that the characteristics of the papers produced at Donside exactly matched those from Sittingbourne in particular. Production modifications were therefore introduced carefully, incrementally and almost imperceptibly but with complete success. Other trials provided the small development team with a clear picture of the quality limits possible with the coating materials and application methods then available. This knowledge was invaluable later when the coater was redesigned for the manufacture of higher-quality grades.

The progress of coating development was not always smooth however. On one occasion A. F. (Sandy) Wakeford (the coating development manager) was involved with a batch of trial material which, when agitated, went almost solid and stalled the agitator. On informing the Production Manager of this he was advised to obtain a shovel and dig the coating out of the 500-gallon vessel it was occupying. People visiting the mill for some time afterwards were surprised to learn that 'digger' Wakeford was a true Aberdonian, with a strong local accent, and not antipodean. This incident apart the contribution Sandy has made in coating development over the past twenty-five years has been of inestimable value.

Paper inspection.

In an effort to provide the mill with identifiable products two grades were launched under the brand name Consort in the early 1970s, a bulky blade-coated mechanical paper which was used in children's annuals, gardening and cookery year books and similar publications. Consort Bulky Blade, as it was named, was sold mainly to D. C. Thomson in Dundee.

The second development was Consort Label, a woodfree paper coated on one side only and used for labelling the contents of cans and bottles. Previous, somewhat sporadic, attempts to manufacture label paper had been made at Sittingbourne but without too much success. The grade was difficult to make and was much less profitable than grades coated on both sides. Printing demands for label papers were stringent. On some subjects ten colours were used requiring three paper passes through a four-colour press. To obtain good registration in these conditions, paper stability of the highest order is essential. Label paper, being coated on one side only, is inherently asymmetric in character and special precautions are necessary to ensure satisfactory printing performance. Donside commenced manufacture with some trepidation but with the knowledge that, if successful, there was a considerable market for the product. Mill technical staff visited customers to ascertain exact requirements and later to monitor paper performance.

Label printers, conservative by nature and habit, took time to be convinced that the paper performed, that the mill could meet tight delivery schedules from Aberdeen to the north west of England and that it would continue to manufacture the grade on a long-term basis. To meet the stringent delivery requirements the mill relied heavily on Munro's Transport, an Aberdeen based family haulage business headed at the time by Duncan Munro snr. Munro had been transporting paper for Donside since the early 1950s when road haulage was denationalised. The company had followed a policy of heavy investment for vehicle replacement and fleet expansion. It was one of the first to introduce innovative arrangements for overnight trunking of loads to main centres of population, particularly London and Manchester. This, allied with drivers specialising in local deliveries (shunters), ensured a guaranteed next-day service from Aberdeen.

Building Donside's reputation for quality and service was exemplified by the experience of George Robins, the Bowater sales representative in whose area most of the label printers were situated. His visits to B. Taylor, a long-established family firm of label printers, were always typified by spirited exchanges with John Bramwell, the Managing Director. George made one visit early in 1970 to find that 20 tonnes of label paper, supplied from Bowaters Sittingbourne, had been rejected. John Bramwell, not known for mincing his words, was volcanic in his criticism of the poor performance of the paper. George listened politely and, at a suitable moment, said 'Mr Bramwell, Bowaters have just acquired a mill in Aberdeen which is specialising in blade coated label papers. You really should try their paper because, in the future, you will eventually buy most of your requirements from them.' John responded 'Well if that's the case we had better have a look at this mill of yours.' A visit to Donside was arranged and John Bramwell made it clear to the mill team, in his familiar uncompromising terms, that quality, performance and service had to be of the highest order or there was no future in any commercial relationship. But he went on to say that 'If you satisfy the requirements of B. Taylor then I will be your best ambassador and salesman amongst the label printers around Manchester and Liverpool.' The mill met the searching demands he made and John Bramwell was as good as his word in publicising Consort Label. George Robins's prediction was also correct – the mill has enjoyed the bulk of the business from B. Taylor for over twenty years.

Paper reel in transit.

The development of label paper was an important milestone for the mill. It demonstrated that, uniquely within the Consortium, it had the resources to make a technically demanding grade. It also helped establish Donside's reputation for service, presentation and delivery. Crucially this grade provided a bedrock foundation for the order book in future years, finding a more reliable demand, even in poor economic conditions, compared with two-sides coated papers. George Robins was close to becoming a dedicated Donside salesman in those early days and it was because of his contacts, his patient manner and knowledge of the label business that the mill gained and still retains a pre-eminent market share. It is quite possible that, without Consort Label, the mill might not have survived in the severe recession of 1975.

A superior quality art paper was also developed. Sales were modest, deliberately limited to a single merchant, under the brand name Queen of Scots. But although sales did not set the heather on fire it was invaluable experience. It helped to open the way to enhanced quality and was the basis for the establishment of art grades later in the 1980s.

Competition for the UK coated papers market came mainly from European mills which were visited by Donside executives to assess relative technical competence, production efficiency and to establish benchmarks against which future performance could be judged. After one such visit made to mills in Germany and Denmark in December 1971 the Donside mill and production managers reported thus:

> Even allowing for the larger runs, fewer grade changes and generally higher average paper substance it is clear that the operating broke (wastage) percentages are substantially below the norm in the UK. Whereas the Consortium mills may be high in the domestic efficiency league, looking towards Europe it is apparent that there they would be second division operators at the present time.

At Donside a programme was immediately started to narrow the efficiency gap with Europe.

As this programme took effect the output potential of the mill increased. This served to underline the problems of operating in the overflow mode established by the Consortium agreement. Higher operating efficiencies on the newer papermachine meant more idle time on No. 1 machine. Capital expenditure limitations had placed pressure on the cutting/sheeting sections and the existing equipment and conversion personnel squeezed output to the limit. Once, a cutter operator, asked why a particular order had not been finished, responded 'After all Rome was not built in a day.' The reply was 'That's only because Jim Munro (the day conversion superintendent) wasn't in charge.'

The layout of finishing and conversion equipment was modified to improve the flow of paper between processes. Conveyor handling was installed to avoid transporting paper by lift to the conversion section situated above the coater/finishing house. To achieve this required the resiting of all paper cutters at machine-floor level. This phased programme took many years to achieve but consequent savings in labour costs and reduction in handling damage made the effort well worth while.

The prolonged and deep recession of 1975–6 had a devastating impact on the industry. Donside operated only one machine for a continuous period of 22 months. Rigid limits were placed on all expenditure and the total mill complement fell to a low of 374. It was a very tough time for the paper industry generally and a number of mills were permanently shut down. Donside survived – just.

Towards the end of 1976 the mill General Manager, John Fedo, was asked to return to manage Bowaters Mersey Mill, which was also in severe difficulty. He was reluctant to leave Donside and the management team with whom he had enjoyed an excellent and productive relationship but eventually accepted the appointment. In October of that year he was succeeded as General Manager at Donside by Ian Lakin.

The year following saw some improvement in activity levels. However, for Donside, a much more important event was the decision of Reed International to sell its half share in the mill to the other Consortium partner for £1,100,000.

CHAPTER NINE

Single Ownership Again

Gates, St Machar's Cathedral

THE REASON GIVEN at the time by Reed International for the disposal of their half share of Donside was 'a further step in the strategy to strengthen Reed's operational base and financial structure'. In the light of events which followed it would seem more likely that the sale was part of the plan to cease papermaking activities eventually and concentrate on publishing and packaging. Later, in mid-1981, they closed Imperial Paper Mill at Gravesend in Kent. This included the blade coater making light-weight mechanical grades.

The Reed Directors resigned from the Donside Board and additional Bowater Directors joined under the chairmanship of Tom Wilding who was also Chairman of Bowater UK Paper Company. Ian Lakin was one of the new appointees to the Bowater Board at this time and, in early 1983, he became Managing Director at Donside.

For the mill the years of unfocused sales strategy suddenly disappeared. The message to the Bowater sales team was 'fill Donside'. Aided by the gradual upturn in demand over the following two years the level of mill activity increased, yielding better profits than had ever been earned previously. By 1981 and into 1982, however, yet another deep recession was decimating British industry. The paper industry suffered greatly, paper machines were shutting at an average rate of one per week, and there were many mill closures. Donside was also affected by the recession but, when the coater at Reed's Imperial Mill ceased production, the mill was able to acquire some of the resulting free tonnage without which their annual loss in 1982 of £732,000, incurred on a turnover of £19.8 million, would have been much greater.

However, the mill management were well aware that the long-term future was still far from secure. At the time 30 per cent of the mill order book was based on lightweight coated (LWC) mechanical grades which yielded relatively low prices. At Imperial, Reed's had already experienced increasingly severe competition from much larger, faster and more cost-efficient machines operating in Sweden and West Germany. It was similar to the newsprint competition of the 1950s all over again but with higher quality paper. The likely fate of the mill was no secret. The LWC tonnage gave the mill some breathing space during which a long-term strategy was discussed and evolved.

The principal objectives of this plan were quite simply expressed:

- Increase sales volume in higher value-added grades
- Obtain agreement for the appointment of a mill-based selling organisation to represent Donside
- Ensure that the mill and its products were brought into sharp focus for prospective customers

Implementing the plan was more difficult and often involved making market, technical and capital spending decisions based on an intuitive 'feel' for the situation. It was appreciated that there was no point in competing in the coated paper market area occupied by Bowaters Sittingbourne. To do so would limit the potential for output growth at both mills. Other market areas would have to be identified. The Bowater Sales Company were reluctant (to say the least) to hive off its recently acquired responsibilities for Donside sales. It took some delicate negotiation by Ian Lakin before a qualified initial agreement was reached by which Donside could employ their own sales team for label paper only.

In late 1982 Andrew Findlay joined the Donside Board as Sales Director. He had worked for Bowater for over 20 years and immediately preceding his appointment to Donside was Bowater Group Export Sales Director. In that capacity he had made a number of visits to the USA and was familiar with the coated paper grade structure and quality requirements in this very large market.

Furthermore Ian Lakin was familiar with the technical ability of many coating mills in the USA where he had been a consultant to a chemical

company developing alkaline sizing. This was based on the earlier experience which had been gained in this field over the previous twelve years at Donside. Cliff Kirk, the mill Technical Manager, had made a substantial contribution to the introduction and practical application of this technology. By this time the benefits were well known as was the fact that it was the keystone in attempting the production of higher specification coated papers. However, since American coated mills had not attempted alkaline sizing, Donside held a significant lead.

By mid-1982 the USA was leading the Western economies out of the deep recession of the previous two years. Export opportunities for all grades of coated papers emerged. At Donside the coater had been modernised and revised coating heads had been installed. The mill team had developed, in-house, the vital technique for applying high coat weights of the sophisticated formulations essential to achieve the higher gloss and smoothness specifications for the No. 1 grade in the American market.

During one of their joint visits Ian Lakin and Andrew Findlay were emphatically advised by American paper merchants that they would consider selling coated papers on behalf of Donside only if the mill offered a complete range of substances. Lakin broke off from the remainder of the tour and returned to Aberdeen. Immediately he organised mill trials and, within weeks, the maximum substance capability of No. 1 machine was increased from 170g/m^2 to 270g/m^2. No mean effort!

As a result agreements were concluded with two major independent paper merchants in the USA – Ris in the North East and Kirk in California. The merchants' requirements for paper packing, in cartons, and damage-free shipping in containers were also assimilated. Aided by the pound/dollar ratio, which was favourable to exporters at the time, the new arrangements rapidly generated profitable sales. The brand name given by the Americans to the range was Gleneagle – a happy association with the time they had spent at a certain internationally celebrated hotel in Perthshire!

The pound/dollar ratio was not however favourable in every respect, as Ian Lakin found when he was booked into the Waldorf Hotel in New York at a nightly rate of $300. As the pound was worth 98 cents at the time Ian's sense, as an Aberdonian, of good value was outraged. It is not recorded whether he took the hotel breakfast for which there was an additional charge.

Success in the USA was repeated at home in two ways. In mid-1983 Wiggins Teape PLC decided to cease production of the high quality coated art papers and boards at their Stoneywood Mill in Aberdeen. On learning of this decision Ian Lakin and Jim O'Connor (Donside's Commercial Director following Gilbert Urquhart's retirement) opened up negotiations with Ed Gillespie, General Manager at Stoneywood, who had previously worked at Donside in the late 1960s and 1970s, and Henry Green, their Marketing

Director. It was agreed that Donside would take on production of Wiggins Teape's coated art papers and that production of the heavyweight board range would be handled by Tullis Russell of Markinch, Fife. The complete range would be branded and sold by Wiggins Teape PLC. This swift local action prevented the permanent loss of valuable tonnage to foreign mills.

Donside also made the high quality papers for a number of paper merchants who marketed them under their own brand name. This increased mill sales tonnage but had the disadvantage that Donside's identity was obscured by the merchant's brand name.

The timing and judgement as well as intuition exercised in these moves into higher value-added grades brought its reward when, following the loss made in 1982, turnover rose in 1983 to £23.2 million and in 1984 to £32.7 million. Profit for the respective years increased to £911,000 and £2.5 million – a mill record at that time.

Determined to identify the mill with high-quality paper in the domestic market the company decided to withdraw from the scheme by which merchants branded Donside paper under their own name. This was very unpopular with the merchant houses when notice was given in late 1986. The mill-branded ranges, Consort Royal Art and Consort Royal Satin, were launched on 1 January 1987. For the merchants the impact of the move was softened with the offer of franchises for the mill range. The mill undertook marketing, technical back-up and provided other preferential services to this group of specialists in coated art papers.

Development of Label paper continued. It still constituted a vital segment of the order book with the mill holding 35 per cent of the home market. Printing on six-colour presses running at high speed became commonplace. Canning and bottling line operating speeds increased dramatically. These developments put further demands on paper performance which the mill duly satisfied.

Smoothness and gloss of Donside's Label paper were further improved and the mill ran ahead of the market requirement for a time when it was decided to install a third coating head on the Highland Chief. This enabled two layers of coating to be applied to one side of the sheet, giving the superior printing quality essential for prestige products like Scotch whisky and higher-quality food labels. The expertise coating 'blade-on-blade' on one side of the sheet thus obtained was used to move further up-market into the production of Real Art two-side coated papers. This marked Donside's entry into a small and exclusive group of mills in the top echelon of coated paper manufacturers world wide of which three, including Donside, were in Europe.

CHAPTER TEN

Real Art

Woodside Fountain

MEETING THE DEMANDING specification for Real Art coated paper requires the highest standards of base-paper uniformity. Two applications of coating per side are necessary. The base sheet is precoated with exactly the correct material to prepare the paper for the second coat. The second coat contains the special pigments and adhesives which endow the surface with the very high gloss and smoothness which is the hallmark of Real Art grades. The coating formulations must be designed to ensure that, after printing, the inks maintain their lustre and the subject retains the life and contrast required by the graphic designer. When Real Art is specified the subjects concerned, whether they be programmes for an important event, corporate literature or fine books, invariably are intended to convey an image of prestige and excellence. Only the highest quality and performance standards are acceptable.

The coater used to initiate the development into Real Art was not equipped with four application heads (two for each side of the base paper). Thus, in order to double coat for trial purposes, it was necessary to pass the paper twice through the coater. This tended to disrupt normal production and was time consuming, but the results obtained were encouraging. The decision to equip the coater with the additional (fourth) application head was not easy. As Ian Lakin explained:

> The mill operated only one coater and produced a wide range of substances of one-side coated papers (label) as well as two-side grades. To enter the specialised and sophisticated world of Real Art would further diversify the manufacturing techniques placing additional demands on operators. However, we had a knowledgeable and adaptable workforce. It was also important that the volume of orders for the new grade should give sufficiently long production runs to achieve the absolute uniformity required in the finished product.

After careful consideration the decision was taken to commit the requisite considerable investment and go into production. The fourth coating-head was ordered and installed. When this project was completed during the mill annual maintenance shutdown in 1989 the Highland Chief was over twice its original (1967) length. It was provided with a range of fully proven sensors to measure and control coat weight, profile and moisture as well as a variety of modern drying techniques and sophisticated flying splice equipment.

In the week before start up it was learnt that the only other mill in the UK producing Real Art was to cease manufacture of papers manufactured using blade-on-blade coating techniques. The reason given was that it had not proved possible to maintain regularly the high quality standards demanded of Real Art. Recalling the situation later Ian Lakin observed 'That news was

Paper stock chest with agitator.

Inspection of base paper.

not very encouraging but, on reflection, it meant that there was substantial tonnage to pick up provided we met the quality standards quickly.'

The Real Art range was launched in mid-1989 again under the brand name Consort Royal. It comprised papers to three specifications:

Brilliance – the high gloss version

Silk – with a very smooth surface but without high gloss

Silk Tint – a cream shade having the surface characteristics of Silk

At the time Wiggins Teape Merchants were seeking a supplier of Real Art papers to extend their portfolio of coated grades. Following the launch Donside had quickly achieved the required specification for Real Art and this, together with the success of the previous arrangement for the supply of Consort Royal Art and Satin, persuaded Wiggins Teape to contract for the supply of the complete new range including the coated boards.

The American merchants were not forgotten and, on being offered the new grade, decided to market under the Donside brand names in preference to their own.

These three opportunities quickly established for the mill what was aptly described by Ian Lakin as 'a strong presence on the hallowed ground of the Real Art market'. Sales volume was sufficient to generate adequate manufacturing runs for product uniformity together with any fine tuning required.

Real Art occupied only a small segment of the total market for coated papers so the mill realised that, truly to establish its position, the product must have appeal in the global market which included Europe and Japan as well as the USA and UK. Merchants and agents were appointed in Denmark,

Holland, Belgium and, in the face of considerable local opposition, Germany and France. With promotional support from the mill these merchants are now accounting for 50 per cent of all exports of Real Art and other papers, including Label, from the mill.

Promotions in the domestic market are targeted increasingly towards graphic designers who specify papers on behalf of the end customer. Recognising the influential position of both designer and printer, Donside organise a prestigious annual competition for graphic design and printing excellence. Entries, in a number of categories in print and design, are judged and awards made by independent and respected industry specialists. Following the awards the winning entries are exhibited and later published in booklet form. Originally the competition was domestic but now international entries are encouraged, reflecting the global scope for the mill's Real Art papers. There is just one entry condition – entries must be made on Donside paper!

The successful introduction of Real Art to the mill product range marked the attainment of the long-term objective, undertaken in the early 1980s, to increase volume and move to higher value-added grades. A comparison of

Munro lorry (in Donside livery) at the mill awaiting loading.

Munro's off-site storage facility: Donside paper in store.

sales and production figures for each period reveals the significance of the achievement.

Grade	1980–81	1990–91
Light-weight coated	13,784 Te	nil
Consort Label	13,142 Te	23,487 Te
Consort Royal Art range	nil	25,694 Te
Other coated grades	12,500 Te	11,864 Te
TOTAL SALES	39,426 Te	61,045 Te
TRADING PROFIT	£320,000	£5,200,000

Because this development concerned grades unique to Donside, the mill sales organisation, headed by Andrew Findlay, now deals exclusively with all the mill products, promotions and customer servicing for the home and international markets.

The increased volume and diversity of products necessitated a fundamental review of stock holding and distribution facilities. Finished paper storage space at the mill was very limited. An agreement was negotiated with the mill's transport contractor, Munro, now led by Duncan jnr., by which they set up a separate arm of their company to deal with storage and distribution. They provided warehouse space for cut and

Above: *Dandy Roll, No. 2 machine.*

Facing page: *Section of Highland Chief.* Inset: *Paper reel.*

wrapped paper on pallets and also reels. A number of storage sites in the vicinity of Aberdeen were equipped to unload trailers from the mill, store and subsequently distribute paper to customers as required by the mill. Previously Munro had delivered empty trailers for loading by the mill personnel and then collected them for delivery to customers in the UK. Up to this point they had not been involved with any paper handling.

With the new arrangement Munro had to train their own operators in the skills of safe, damage-free paper handling, storage and retrieval. To improve communication and inventory control their main warehouses were connected to the mill computer system. Another service taken on by Munro was loading of containers for export. Packing and protection routines were developed to ensure safe transit across the Atlantic.

In the period from the time that Bowater had acquired Reed's share in the mill in late 1977 until the early 1990s Donside had, as we have seen, implemented fundamental change. The quality of its products had been fundamentally improved and production volume more than doubled. This had been matched by an equally bold and radical approach to the market. The mill entered its centenary year established as a profitable leader in an élite area of the industry.

Lippke
DANGER
Radiation risk
THIS LIPPKE GAUGE
CONTAINS 2 RADIOACTIVE
SOURCES
Fe55 3·7G Bq
Kr85 14·8G Bq
SHUTTER OPEN
SHUTTER CLOSED
CONTROLLED AREA
RADIATION

CHAPTER ELEVEN

Management Buy-Out and New Owners

Town House, Old Aberdeen

THE SUCCESS OF the late 1970s and 1980s could not have been achieved without notable consistency of management and strategic policy. Yet this took place in the context of major changes in ownership.

After 1977, when they had acquired the total equity of Donside, Bowater became increasingly disenchanted with paper manufacture. In 1980 they shut down their main newsprint operation at Mersey Mill at Ellesmere Port, Cheshire, which had been losing money at an alarming rate. This left them with three papermaking sites – at Kemsley and Sittingbourne in Kent and at Donside in Aberdeen. Taken together the paper activities produced only a marginal profit on turnover. In 1985 the return on sales of £154 million was £1.4 million, pretty unexciting stuff!

As the 1980s progressed Tom Wilding, who was chairman of Bowater UK Paper Company, became aware that, 'A parting of the ways was going to occur. It seemed that Bowater did not want to continue in the paper business.' In 1985 he began serious discussion with the Corporation with the aim of bidding to buy out the papermaking division.

In September 1986 after 'extraordinarily complex negotiations' the sale was agreed at a purchase price of £38.7 million. A team of seventy senior managers from the three mills made personal investments totalling £400,000 in the new company which was named simply UK Paper. Tom Wilding became Chairman of the new company and the Managing Directors of the three mills also joined the Board. The main shareholders were Electra and Globe Investment Trusts with 70 per cent and Scandanavian Bank with 10 per cent of the equity.

Commentators considered the deal to be favourable to the new owners since more than £20 million had been invested in new and replacement equipment in the two years preceding the buy-out.

Each mill continued as an independent profit centre. Thus Donside still maintained a separate identity and contributed substantial profit in each of the subsequent years.

In February 1988 an offer for sale was announced involving 29,477,944 ordinary 10p shares of UK Paper at an offer price of £1.35 each. A number of shares were reserved for employees and these were fully taken up. The flotation was successful and the public issue was oversubscribed. In effect the value of the company had increased to £107.6 million in less than 18 months. Those managers who had participated in the buy-out had been handsomely rewarded.

The trading results for 1988 showed a profit of 8.7 per cent on turnover, a significant improvement on the last year with Bowater. The share price

Paper cutting at the guillotine.

Pulp bale storage area and boiler house chimney.

improved accordingly and traded between £2.60 and £2.80 in late 1989. But this was not enough in Tom Wilding's view. He spoke of his concern to various trade and financial journals. He considered that, 'The share price should be higher because of the enhanced value of the company's landholdings worth £45 million and also the danger that the company was vulnerable to predators.'

Whether or not Wilding intended his public comments to attract potential buyers is not clear but, within weeks, in November 1989 a bid for UK Paper was received from Metsa Serla, a large Finnish pulp and paper company. Metsa bid £3.30 per share valuing UK Paper at £263 million. This offer was

Cutter reel store.

accepted by the directors and recommended to the shareholders. Financial analysts considered the bid to be too low and, within three weeks, Fletcher Challenge had entered the fray.

They offered £3.75 per share, valuing the company at £298 million. Again the directors recommended the offer to the shareholders and by early January 1990 Fletcher Challenge had gained 50.6 per cent of the share capital and control of the company. Fletcher is the largest industrial company in New Zealand and has world wide interests in pulp and paper. The acquisition of UK Paper represented Fletcher's first investment in Europe which it perceived as a large and potentially lucrative market for paper, with prices which were expected to hold up better than the prices for market pulp, a sector in which Fletcher had a high exposure.

After the acquisition all the UK Paper directors remained to run the company for the new owners. For Donside little perceptible change was noticed and in any event many mill personnel were preoccupied with the considerations surrounding the impending launch of the Real Art grades in July 1989, discussed in the previous chapter.

While the management of the UK operation was not subject to central control from New Zealand changes in style became apparent. There was greater emphasis on personal development and training. Performance comparisons were made on an international basis and benchmarks established. Best practice world wide was sought and implemented. In the UK in-group competition gave way to greater co-operation and free exchange of information.

When Tom Wilding retired as Chairman of UK Paper his successor, Monty August, thoroughly endorsed the new philosophy. Until recently he had Ian Lakin as his deputy. Lakin was based in Aberdeen and retained his managing directorship of Donside Paper Company. This he combined with his role as Operations Director for all three mills – which required frequent visits to Kent.

Although he spent less time at Donside Lakin was nevertheless the prime mover for development in that mill which 'Must be kept moving forward to maintain its position amongst the best coating mills in the world'. In July 1993 he was appointed Senior Vice-President, Business Development (North America) for Fletcher Challenge reporting directly to the Chief Executive's Office in New Zealand.

CHAPTER TWELVE

Paper for the Next Century

St Machar's Cathedral

HAVING ESTABLISHED DONSIDE in the highest quality echelon of coated paper manufacture there could be no standing still to admire the achievement. There was more to be done.

Reacting to customer preference a complete range of environmental papers has been developed. These use TCF pulps which are free of the chlorine normally employed in the bleaching process. In addition a proportion of recycled wastepaper is included in the base-paper furnish. Marketed under the brand name Consort Royal Osprey the range exactly mirrors and complements the Real Art and Consort Royal Art and Satin grades. There is a slight reduction in sheet brightness but in all other respects performance is identical. Consort Royal Osprey grades now account for 30 per cent of all Real Art sales.

Donside aimed to expand its presence in the USA beyond the North-Eastern seaboard which was the principal area covered by Ris, the merchant with which the mill had been associated for some ten years. After some amicable discussions with Howard Ris it was agreed that Donside would acquire the agency segment of the business from Ris since he did not wish to

Paper cutter.

expand in this direction. UK Paper (North America) was formed and Donside appointed the President and Vice-President. This unit has now appointed seven additional merchants to sell the Donside coated-paper range. Ris continue with their merchants' agreement and activities as before.

At the mill efforts to formalise the administration and practice of product quality control and assurance has been recognised by the award of British Standard 5750 Part 2 certification. It was particularly appropriate that the award was made on behalf of BSI by Brenda Dean, the National Secretary of the Union representing papermaking employees. The philosophy and practice of quality assurance relies heavily on the wholehearted acceptance and operation of the system by the workforce.

An important requirement of BS 5750 relates to continuing training and education. Considerable investment has been devoted to in-house training of operators at all levels. Donside together with all the other Aberdeen mills are very fortunate to have easy access to the full range of paper technology education provided by the Robert Gordon University (formerly Robert Gordon's Institute of Technology) in Aberdeen. The Paper Technology Unit was set up in 1961 and has provided a sound, comprehensive papermaking education to a generation of production trainees, engineers and managers

Facing page: *The modern Super Calender, capable of exerting a pressure of one tonne per inch-width of paper.*

B' CAL

Trimmed paper stacked ready for packing.

not only for the local mills but also for the remainder of the UK industry and some overseas mills as well.

Courses specific to local needs are organised and well supported. Recently a steering committee has been formed, chaired at present by Ian Lakin, who is a Governor of the Robert Gordon University, and comprises academic representatives and the General Managers of the local and Scottish mills. It also includes the Director of Education and Training of the British Paper and

Board Industry Federation. Its aim is to ensure that close liasion between industry needs and academic output is maintained through formal lines of communication.

A number of the graduates recruited by Donside have attended RGU to gain a wider familiarity with the basics of all paper-manufacturing techniques prior to taking up their mill duties and filling key positions in the future. The mill team has been augmented over the years by a small number of appointments dedicated to ensuring that technical advances are maintained and the increasing work load handled efficiently.

Despite the changes in ownership the mill management team has remained virtually unaltered. Each of the senior managers in the vital areas of Finance, Production, Product Development, Conversion, Engineering and Personnel have held their appointments for many years, most of them since the new management team was established following the take-over by the Consortium in 1969. In the same period there have been only two mill general managers. The stability thus created allied to their cumulative experience has been a significant factor in the progress and success achieved. The question of succession will no doubt be addressed in the next few years, but the existing team will be a hard act to follow.

The workforce has also made a significant contribution to the mill's success. At times it has demanded convincing arguments before acceptance of new proposals but progress has never been impeded. The mill management has not always followed established practice in working and shift rota arrangements. Agreements have been negotiated which reflect the particular requirements of the mill and the available equipment. Key supervisors and operators in many areas of the mill have long experience and can offer much in practical input when development trials are converted into production practice. Paying tribute to their adaptability and dedication Ian Lakin says, 'The quality of our workforce is fundamental to the mill's success. In recognition of this we are currently seeking more effective ways of using this key asset.'

Many of the policies evolved following the Consortium takeover are still in place. For instance, capital expenditure has always been financed internally from revenue thus avoiding nasty surprises when interest rates soar on external borrowings, a factor which has seen the demise of many businesses during the current recession. The past fifteen years has seen virtually a new mill emerge with replacement and additional plant in all areas. As well as the coater and papermachine developments, a new stock preparation plant has been built. To meet the requirements both of increased production and the customer a new single-drum winder and new cutters incorporating the most modern technical advances have been purchased.

The philosophy behind the capital spending required that each increment of investment must produce the projected reduction in cost or increase in

The Donside Paper Company Limited Board, spring 1993. Back row (left to right): Bruce Stuart (Chief Engineer), Alistair Dinnie (Personnel Manager), Cliff Kirk (Technical Manager), Tom Spiers (Product Manager), George McIntosh (Information Technology Manager). Seated (left to right): Jim O'Connor (Commercial Director), Ian Lakin (Managing Director), Andrew Finlay (Sales and Marketing Director). Below: *Ken Nicholson (Conversion Manager).*

revenue so as to contribute to the financing of succeeding developments. Purchases of equipment have been made on the basis of excellence, technical merit and specific suitability for the intended purpose. This policy has often unfortunately necessitated purchases from outside the UK – essential in the circumstances to maintain the company's position in a highly competitive world market.

The result of the programme of steady investment allied to product development is a mill which produces in excess of 80,000 tonnes of highest quality coated paper with a workforce of 545. To put this in perspective, in 1968 barely 20,000 tonnes were made with a workforce of 629, with the same number of papermachines and the single coater.

What will the future hold? Certainly increased production: this is already planned and will optimise the present papermachines/coater output at approximately 90,000 tonnes. Thereafter a second coater is a possibility, the older paper machine could be replaced and total future output would exceed 150,000 tonnes. Product improvement will continue to maintain the position in the top echelon of mills making Real Art papers. Whatever happens, one thing is certain – Donside has demonstrated ability to survive (despite a few excursions to the edge of the precipice!), absorb changes in ownership, innovate and develop.

The past decade has seen more fundamental change and growth at Donside than in the whole of its previous distinguished history. Thus it continues a fine tradition for quality paper founded by Patrick Sandilands on the banks of the Don at the dawn of the eighteenth century. It is a pretty good bet that the Mill will see that tradition flourish well into the twenty-first.

Index

The Merket Cross